YKRA

Kilian Schönberger

The Outsiders

New Outdoor Creativity

gestalten

**796.
502
8
OUT**

"Between every two pine trees there is a door leading to a new way of life." *John Muir*

Spending time in nature is a humbling and inspiring experience. From the adventurer who sets out to conquer the highest peaks and overcome the greatest of physical challenges to a group of friends sitting around the glowing warmth of a campfire on a cold fall night, there are endless opportunities to enjoy our vast and open landscapes. In previous times, a true outdoor lifestyle was a choice that few made. Not everyone has the resolve to climb a towering mountain to reach the summit in the upper limits of our atmosphere or turn their back completely on civilization, seeking permanent solitude and isolation deep in the wild. But now this lifestyle reaches more and more people who depart from places like Portland, Berlin, or Osaka to step into nature. The desire to be outdoors comes, most probably, from our ever increasing busy lifestyles with little time to relax and little space to move in. Nature is offering herself as the solution to these modern-day problems. It is no wonder the outdoor movement is thriving, now more than ever.

A once common stereotype that is associated with outdoor enthusiasts is that they are of the older generation, raised in a time when being outside was their only source of entertainment. They grew up learning a different type of skill set in stark contrast to the modern generation. What we are seeing in the rise of the outdoor urbanites is a different set of expectations from nature to those of the older generation: the urbanite is looking to re-connect with the outdoors having never experienced it before. The urbanites are starting to develop an independence from their dependence on the modern day, purposely seeking out opportunities to do so.

There is a dream that is shared amongst many of these people, a dream where they can remove themselves from their inner-city dwellings, disconnect from the world, turning off emails and iPhones in exchange for a simpler environment, a wooden cabin with only the forest for company. It is a life that many long for, and it could explain the rise in nature's presence in contemporary culture today.

The simplicity of an outdoor lifestyle is one that has been portrayed as an overly romantic way to live your life, connecting us back to how people lived in the "good old days." But however you want to enjoy the outdoors, whether by capturing the retro chic of Edmund Hillary through the gear you wear or by embarking on an adventure with gadgetry and modern hi-tech equipment that can save your life, there is no set of rules other than to respect and enjoy the outdoors.

As a platform to share our ideas, the role of nature seems to be used to express freedom and in some cases raise awareness of the exploits of modern living. But for some nature is more than this: it is a way of life, first and foremost, and their output is an extension of this lifestyle. Andrew Groves is an example of a contemporary creative who lives and works in the outdoors, situated in a converted barn in the forest. His surroundings are the basis for his creative output. His illustrative work is filled with references to his lifestyle. But what is interesting about Andrew's case is that his real passion lies within the forest itself, creating and crafting wooden tools from the very forest he lives in.

Funded initially through Kickstarter, Andrew runs wood-carving workshops under the guise of Miscellaneous Adventures. He is inviting his followers to come into his world and experience creativity in a different way. Using platforms like Kickstarter and Twitter to generate the funding needed to get his project up and running is a clear indicator that there is an eagerness from the creative community to get up from behind their screens, don their plaid shirts, and head into the forest to learn a skill that is timeless. Andrew's workshops are just a small example of the growing support for opportunities like this. The passion for the outdoors is gaining a momentum that is creating a platform of opportunities for larger projects to take place, products to be developed, and brands to form.

An adventure is something that has endless starting points, but it is the spirit of adventure itself that begins them all. It is defined by an experience that excites and challenges us and nature kindly offers herself as the playground for us to live out our adventure, no matter how big or small it may be. It is the possibilities and the starting points that hold the most excitement: the anticipation of zipping up your wetsuit and paddling out into the early morning waves, spotting your line before dropping into a meter of fresh "pow," unfolding a map and plotting a route, chalking your hands up before that first move, packing your bag and loading the van, looking up from the bottom unable to see the top, peering out of the tent on a fresh spring morning to the very first step on your first hike. These feelings you get just before you start are what keeps outdoor enthusiasts coming back day after day looking for the next adventure.

Be Prepared

Some of the most inspiring people today are using adventures and the outdoors as a platform to showcase what is possible in our hectic lifestyles if we allow ourselves that opportunity to step into nature. These people are inspiring others to go out there and seek their own adventures, and with the right mindset it is possible for the solo hiker or the collective of friends to do so. Nature is a place though that can be very unforgiving to the unprepared. As the urban outsiders embark on their trips, there are certain pieces of equipment that might save their lives, and more commonly there are the creature comforts which are ever present in our packs.

When heading outdoors there are several elements of survival that every adventurer needs to address, from the very basics of food, shelter, and water to the more comfortable aspects like staying warm and dry. There are products that have addressed these needs for many years simply because they are good at what they do and can be relied upon in every eventuality. But we are now starting to see a new wave of products, designed entirely to satisfy needs and tastes that were not present before now.

The more time you spend in nature the more experienced you become. The trees and mountains have a wisdom about them that has formed over their long existence and this is true of the brands that have shaped and influenced the outdoor lifestyle today. The heritage of these older more prolific brands is captured in some of the modern day products we see. The classic mountaineering style backpack and the bright orange of the down jackets are a common sight. When we talk about classic outdoor brands whose products are timeless, we are also talking about the equipment they produce that has had a huge and lasting impact on the outdoor lifestyle. The most iconic of outdoor tools is the knife, and most serious outdoor enthusiasts understand the versatility and importance a good knife can have. Opinel began making knives in the 1800s and to this day there are few who do it better. The confidence in carrying equipment that has been crafted with such expertise could make the difference between life and death in the outdoors.

Tradition and experience are key features in the production of any equipment, and when it comes to boots, arguably the most significant product in the outdoors, the wrong fit could potentially ruin a beautiful day out and plague you for an entire trip. Meindl have over 300 years of experience in boot making, the kind of experience that is acquired from miles upon miles of walking. It is this experience and quality that allows them to provide products for the modern outsider.

Clean water is essential for human existence, and in a lot of cases it is no mean feat obtaining a clean water source when you are out in the mountains. More and more, the ways in which we are able to purify water on the go are becoming increasingly simple and effective. When we do not have time to boil a pot of water, we can turn to some of the most sophisticated solutions out there like Sawyer's 0.1 Micron Absolute Water Filters, which can be fitted to most standard water bottles and hydration packs. The longevity of these products is remarkable too: Vapur's Eclipse MicroFilter is able to purify hundreds of liters of water from lakes, rivers, and streams in a handheld water pouch.

As simple a life we wish to lead, there are still modern necessities that not everyone can live without. Fortunately we have companies that are creating solutions to help the urbanites survive with some of the common amenities of the twenty-first century. The most important urban survival tool of today is the mobile phone. It is almost as if it contains the very thing that keeps people alive and without it they cannot go on. BioLite is a company that embraces the dependence we have on modern technology in some truly remarkable ways. You can power your phone from the heat that the fire inside their BioLite CampStove generates, which is transported as electricity to a USB port for charging devices at the same time you are heating up a meal or coffee to recharge yourself.

A Love Affair With Nature

With the new wave of urban adventurers there are opportunities for new problems to be solved and new products to be created for this growing market. The key to any product is that it is functional, especially in the outdoors where it is relied upon to perform without fault. Unlike most brands, where the brand most often precedes the products, an outdoor brand has a responsibility to meet the demands that you would expect of functioning equipment. Without this it is likely not to survive in this market for long. If the product is reliable and can withstand the demands of the outdoors, then the brand story has the platform to share the honesty that is quite often found within the outdoor market.

This honesty runs through outdoor brands the world over. Set up by passionate outdoor enthusiasts, they provide equipment that is a true reflection of their love affair with nature. What makes these brands different from any other movement is that they are inviting you in to be part of their lifestyle. The products and ethos of the brands are steeped in experience but refrain from judgment of your ability and come with the encouragement needed to set you out on your next adventure.

The brands and consumers today all have a responsibility when it comes to the preservation of nature and the resources it takes to manufacture the equipment we rely on. In the wild it is good practice to leave behind no trace you were ever there, and this mindset should also be carried through when it comes to products. The responsibility of the consumer is about smart purchasing, questioning their need for the latest season's Gore-Tex jacket, caring for the products they do purchase, and understanding how their purchase will impact the environment they will inevitably want to enjoy.

The brands of course have a bigger responsibility when it comes to the environment. One thing that the outdoor market is known for is the lifespan of a product. Used time and time again, classic items like the Stanley thermos flask are passed down and shared through generations of outdoor trips. The quality of production is important in any of the products and it is all to easy for mother nature to expose any weakness. So for any of the brands the primary focus should be on the production of durable equipment.

The outdoor market is a playground for innovation, from an extensive array of materials and fabrics being developed to withstand the most extreme of conditions, to the shape and style of boards and skis to create a better riding experience. Brands like Fjällräven have developed their own eco-friendly fabric: the G-1000 series is a hybrid of durable performance fabric designed with a classic lasting appeal. It is these kinds of hybrid eco products that are the future of the outdoor market. With savvy outdoor consumers who are able to digest a lot of information about a product before they purchase anything, it is important that both the product and the brand are standing up to the test.

The functionality of the products is sometimes, however, missed by the everyday wearer. As we are seeing more and more outdoor clothing in the streets of our cities, the products are not always being put to use in their natural environment. They are in many cases bought to mimic that outdoor feeling for those who have rarely, if ever, left the city. The true test for these brands is whether they can perform in either environment. Once the urbanite leaves the city for the outdoors the gear needs to prove its point when it comes to its natural functions to protect us from the elements.

All these brands, new and old, have a responsibility to nature and the resources of the planet. For humans to go on enjoying the outdoors, we must work towards preserving its life and well being. The outdoor lifestyle's most prominent brand Patagonia is a company that has set the precedent for any business, outdoors or not, to committing to the preservation of the environment. One of their most recent campaigns took the form of a quite blunt message about their own products, "Don't buy this jacket," in an attempt to deter buying for buying's sake, engaging its consumer into questioning the impact of their purchase on the environment. Founder of Patagonia, Yvon Chouinard, also established Patagonia Works, where he is openly offering to invest in any start-up business that has a like-minded responsibility to bring benefits to the environment. It is clear that those whose lives are reliant on nature want to preserve and protect it for the benefit of every person on earth.

Something Old, Something New

One of the defining brands that has emerged from this new generation of outdoor companies is Poler Stuff. Approaching the outdoors with the energy of a skate company combined with the mindset of the most experienced woodsman, they are without doubt producing some of the most sought after products the urban adventurer must have. From their iconic orange tents to the 3/4-length Napsacks, you can guarantee that their products make a cameo in the majority of outdoor photography being snapped up by the "urbaneers."

Alongside Poler is an abundance of brands, new and old, that are defining this new outdoor movement. There are new start-up brands that are set up by individuals and small collectives of friends, and there are the brands with the history and outdoor heritage who have their foot firmly in the contemporary development of the outdoor scene: these people are passionate about their products and the outdoors.

There are companies and cultures around the world making outdoor products. Some that specialize in backpacks, like, YKRA in Budapest and Sandqvist of Sweden, hold dear the heritage of mountaineering. Also there are brands like Bush Smarts in New York, who produce the tools of survival that are needed on any trip. The brands span every corner of the globe with each country having its own influence on the style and design of the product. If you take the classic Scandinavian style tents of Nordisk in Denmark and compare them to the futuristic hanging tree tens of Tentsile in the U.K. there are products of every shape and size available.

What is striking about these newer brands is their clear focus on the craft of products, the understanding of a product's function, and the sourcing of the material to create them, often as ethical and ecological as possible. Brands such as Topo Designs of Colorado, who tailor-make a huge array of products, take pride in manufacturing in the country they live in. There is a surge in handcrafted items that is hard not to notice. Skilled artisans such as Matt Pierce of Wood & Faulk and the Sanborn Canoe team are crafting with natural materials to produce some simply beautiful pieces of outdoor equipment of both aesthetic and practical value.

All these brands present themselves with an honesty that is very easy for the urban adventurer to aspire to. The simplicity of life is a picture painted so well through these brands that it appears almost too easy to be true, yet astonishingly, it is in fact possible to live out this dream. The products are designed so that there is minimal amount of effort involved when you are setting up your camp before nightfall or paddling across the lake on a summers day. Some companies are making products with the novice in mind. Nature is the simplest of places to be and with the help of brands like Poler and Topo Designs it is possible for each and everyone of us, no matter how urbanized we might be, to become a new-found child of nature.

The encouragement these new brands are instilling in the young urban adventurer is also reflected in the products that they make. A big part of what makes up contemporary culture is the values that we place on aesthetics and style. A lot of thought has clearly gone into the visual styling of the products we see out there and it could be said that this is what is giving more and more people the push they need to step out of the door and head into the mountains. The products, of course, cannot rely on looks alone and must have a level of functionality to them that you would come to expect with an outdoor purchase. But in the same breath they must have a visual appeal that does not alienate the urbanite in the more comfortable surroundings. These are the kinds of demands which new and old brands have to adapt to.

Everyone Is an Adventurer

The Outsiders presents an array of regular people doing exceptional trips through some of the stunning imagery they have captured on their journeys, from the bicycle adventures of Paul and Hansen Hoepner, as they pedal from Berlin to Shanghai across the backcountry roads of the world, to the motorcycle duo of West America's James Crowe and Jordan Hufnagel, with no real plan other than to ride from Canada to Patagonia, letting the unpredictable nature of adventure do the rest.

Some people choose to go solo on their trips while others seek the company of a partner or a group of friends. Sergio Jensen beautifully documents the intimate moments shared with his travelling companions that are common on most trips.It may have once seemed like a male-dominated world but outdoor photographer Anki Grøthe captures the spirit of female adventuring with the series "Nature Ladies" where a group of her friends set off to explore the snowy backyard of their home in Norway.

The adventures do not always have to be ones where extensive physical exertion is involved. Photographer Matt Pensworth captures the spirit of friends enjoying time together in nature, from camping to drifting around in a canoe.

Photography is important when it comes to capturing the spirit of adventure and the beauty of nature. Few do it better than the photographers in *The Outsiders*. Cody Cobb and Kilian Schönberger somehow find a way to make their images of the outdoors feel tangible, finding a balance between the stillness and the overwhelming scale of nature. David Boyson Cooper and Mike Seehagel present the outdoors in such a way that it feels like there is no other way of life but the one they see through their lens, that man was truly meant to live in nature.

What underpins all of the above is creativity. It flows through each and every project and person presented in this book, whether it is a product that has been created to solve a specific problem or the way in which a person has viewed nature to live out their dream adventure, the relationship between nature and creativity is strong. What we are seeing in the movement is how creativity is present in everyone—it is not just in the elite creative, it is an open platform for everyone and a natural flow which we can see.

We are coming back in from the outdoors with a fresh perspective on our lives and our practices. The link between creativity and nature is an obvious one, but it is more than this.It is the effect nature can have on a person's state of mind and outlook which is the most important. We are reconnecting with our history and craft and hopefully preparing for the future with nature as a more present role in our lifestyles.

For me, nature and living an outdoor lifestyle has been the most inspiring presence in my short existence. There is nothing more exciting than seeing now how it is effecting a new generation. There are infinite ways for you to experience the outdoors and hopefully through the pages of this book you will be encouraged enough to take the first of many adventures in the wild or invite others to share your experiences. It is all too easy to be an observer of this movement but to be truly part of it, whichever way you do it, is to take that first step outside.

Jeffrey Bowman is not only an observer of the new outdoor movement, but also an active participant. The graphic designer recently finished an 18-month trip through the mountains of Norway, choosing to leave behind his urbanized lifestyle in pursuit of a simpler way of life. He returns from his adventure ready to begin a new one, establishing his own outdoor brand based in the heart of the English countryside.

"The mountains are calling
and I must go." *John Muir*

We Are All Born Explorers

We are all born explorers. You, me, and everybody else. When I look at my three daughters they are wondering what is hidden behind the next hill, and they did start to climb chairs, stairs, and other stuff before they learned how to walk. My challenge as a father is to make sure they do not stop wondering. Because to be an adventurer is not something you become, it is something you are when you are born. Nobody starts to climb or to do outdoors, it is a natural state of mind. But if you are not very careful in your daily life, you will quit early on. Years of school, parents' expectations and societies different demands slowly grind your original spirit apart, and you eventually start to behave in a civilized way. "In paradise all dreams are made real. Everything is perfect—too perfect.

That is why Adam was thrown out of paradise. He left in order to find challenges and to dream," wrote Arne Næss Jr, leading Norway's first successful Mount Everest expedition in 1985. And my guess is that it was for the same reason Eve was miserable, chose to eat the fruits of the tree of knowledge, and weighed new opportunities. It is said that a lost paradise is the only one that survives time, and that is certainly in accordance with my experiences. Politicians, sociologists, and utopian philosophers dream about the risk-free society. But I agree with my late friend Arne that we humans just are not made for easy solutions only inside buildings and a life with hardly any challenges. The most common question an explorer is asked: "Why do you hike in the forests, walk to the poles, sail across the oceans, and climb the mountains when you can fly?." Why prefer to wake up to −54°C on the pack ice towards the North Pole, why ski to the South Pole in total solitude, or why not rather climb a mountain next to Mount Everest to enjoy the scenery, experience the Sherpa culture, save money, pollute less, and suffer in a lighter fashion? "Because it is there," is of course the most famous answer, and it is a good one because it suggests that it is actually little we have to do in life. I believe Mallory and all his successors primarily travel to Himalaya, Antarctica and the Arctic for everything that is not there and to a lesser degree for what is there. The lack of heat, too little oxygen, pain, and diseases become a part of the enriched feeling of using your potential, being present in your own life, reaching for something which is beyond yourself, and eventually to feel happy.

If most people could do it, then you have to do something which is more challenging. And Mallory's answer is more honest than today's usual named reasons: the raising of money for charity and scientific research, peace, the protection of the environment or vulnerable cultures, and a love for the natural world. It all may be true, but explorers forget their other reasons: egocentricity, a need for attention and recognition, revenge, nationalism, and money. I admit to at least four of these with the exception of nationalism, and I did for many years lose money. But "if you cannot understand that there is something in man which responds to the challenge of this mountain and goes out to meet it, that the struggle is the struggle of life itself upward and forever upward, then you won't see why we go." Mallory goes on: "We do not live to eat and to make money. We eat and make money to be able to live. That is what life means and what life is for." I believe Mallory's state of mind is the original one. To explore is in your DNA. Your first ambition, beyond getting fed, was to reach out beyond yourself, to learn, to experience, to climb. The fact that Mallory never lost this is to me the most fascinating part of him. In a world with so many temptations, so many good and rational reasons for forgetting the child within you, to become a well behaved human being with few proper ambitions, to consume in accordance, and to contribute to the GNP. And to forget that you as a child were happy playing without rules and believed almost everything was possible. There is however one thing that is even more important than it all and seldom mentioned: to explore is a love affair.

And a very strong one. As soon as the idea about becoming the first human to ski to the South Pole alone appeared between my ears I made the decision about doing it and stopped thinking about anything else. It is an absurd thing to do, but love makes you blind. I fell in love with skiing into a white nothingness with everything I needed for the whole expedition on my sled, and as I wrote in my diary, to be able to feel that "Past and future are of no interest. I am living more and more in the present." When you start, the sun's orbit is tilted, it is arced higher in the southern sky and lower in the northern sky. The tilt of the sun's arc gets less and less pronounced as you walk south in the midnight sun. The trip is one long day, and eventually when you get there the sun has the same altitude above the horizon for 24 hours. Antarctica is the coldest place on earth, the windiest and loneliest; it has more hours of sun than Southern California and less precipitation than Western Sahara. A desert made of water. "I can hear and luxuriate in the stillness here. It feels good to be alone in the world," I wrote on day 14. Seven days later I penciled: "At the beginning, everything appeared white and the beauty lay in the endless uniformity. Since then, my senses have developed and my experience of nuances in nature has become ever greater. Flat can also be beautiful."

When I started, everything was white all the way out to the horizon, but as the weeks passed by I started to see more colors: variations of white, a bit blue, red, green, and yellow. I developed a dialog with the environment, threw some thoughts into nature, and got new ideas back. The expedition became more and more a travel into me. I read books that had the maximum number of words and ideas per gram of book weight. And I started to take pleasures from small things, or as I mentioned in my diary on day 22: "At home, I only seem to appreciate 'big bites'. Being down here teaches me to value little pleasures—a nuance in the color of the snow, the wind as it lays itself to rest, a warm drink, and the patterns of the cloud formations. The stillness." "Many people will be jealous, but very few would have been in my place," I thought one of the last days. After 50 days and nights with no radio contact I reached my goal, and on day 49 the diary says: "Just after midnight. 25 km from the South Pole. It is so beautiful I get a lump in my throat. I have felt lonelier at large parties and in big cities than I do here." A feeling and experiences you will never have in a paradise or by flying to your goals because you have to suffer on the way to make your love affair worthwhile.

The Importance of Preparation

Over the years many people have asked me for advice while planning expeditions, and still others have sought guidance on starting on much easier trips. In the light of the questions they ask I am able to get a sense, fairly swiftly, of whether or not they will have bad luck with the weather and other eventualities on the way. Much can be determined before they even set off. I am right away happy to admit that from a completely objective standpoint I have generally been physically weaker and less competent a skier, hiker, sailor, and mountaineer than the majority of others who have done these things. Strictly speaking I have only had one advantage over the herd and that is that I have always been good at preparation. A bit better than some and a lot better than others. In that sense I have had it easier on route. What I have lacked in terms of muscle and native wit, I have tried to make up for by not standing about with my hands in my pockets. And by actually trying instead of giving up. "It is not about the equipment for a journey such as we are about to embark upon. It is not money which brings victory to such an expedition—though, heaven knows, it is good to have—but to a great extent, indeed I believe I daresay first and foremost, the manner in which an expedition is equipped is how each difficulty is anticipated, and how that difficulty is solved or avoided. "Victory awaits he who has all in order—it is called success. For he who has neglected to take the necessary measures, in time failure is absolute certainty—it is called misfortune." These words come from Roald Amundsen's account of how he became the first in history to reach the South Pole. Bold words but accurate nonetheless.

I do not think Amundsen was trying to compare himself with others or slander anyone with his comments. He was just stating a fact: how the day will turn out is well and truly decided even before you leave the tent in the morning, or, for that matter, before anyone starts off on an adventure in the first place. I am often asked if I have been lucky. "If you make it, people will think you were lucky with the weather," was the last thing the Norwegian artist Jakob Weidemann, our main sponsor for the expedition to the North Pole, said to me and my partners Geir Randby and Børge Ousland. I did not think about his remark until after we had come back, and one person after another asked if we had been lucky with the weather. Weidemann was a wise man. There is no point turning to the history of philosophy to learn about luck, because as far as I am aware, luck is not something that is dealt with there. The moral luck of fortune has been a subject of study for years now, but that is something else. Being lucky while doing outdoors is not about being more intelligent than other people or having special physical prowess. On the contrary, luck is about how we behave, it is what we think and feel. Of course it is possible to have pure luck to the extent that one attains something simply as a result of random chance. One of the most famous examples of this kind of luck is Walt Disney's Gladstone Gander from Duckberg in Donald Duck who is always irritatingly and undeservedly fortunate. Another example is Ringo Starr, who was in the right place at the right time. Nonetheless, it is possible to ask just how random coincidence is.

There is a story of a lottery winner who had chosen the number 48 because for 7 nights on the trot he had dreamed of the number 7, and 7 times 7 is 48, right … ? … Well, no actually, but that is the number he gambled on. Consequently it is natural to separate luck one has once in a while from more systematic luck. It is the latter I am interested in. Because it just seems a fact that not only Roald Amundsen but countless others like him are blessed with something resembling good luck. In the same way it would appear that great outdoor people have luck pitching the tent in heavy weather and great sailors luck with the wind. If we consider some of the great global successes—photography, insulin, penicillin, the artificial production of nitrogen, and the contraceptive pill—they are all the result of apparent chance. Ideally I should be prepared for every eventuality, but it is difficult to imagine that being possible. You can plan yourself to death according to the philosopher Seneca. Conditions change, the time I have at my disposal is limited, and each enterprise is dependent on the time available to me to act along the way. Unforeseen and awkward circumstances will arise regardless, but the aim must be to limit them. If I am successful in this respect, it will be possible to have something left over to solve the challenges I did not bargain for, when they arise. Simply deciding what footwear to have with me has been a major task prior to setting out on each expedition.

Heroic Failure

As everyone knows, the head should be kept cold and the feet warm. The great storyteller Hans Christian Andersen was, by all accounts, a man who tried to be prepared for every eventuality while travelling. When he was away, he liked to have with him his own personal fire hose in case a blaze should start where he was staying. Perhaps this sounds rather extreme, because the point is not to attempt to be prepared for absolutely everything. But at the same time there is more to this tale, because in those days fires in hotels were a far greater problem than they are today. The fire brigade, if and when they were to be found at all in a certain place, seldom possessed long ladders. So, on reflection, perhaps it was a sensible precaution after all. All in all it is important to take advantage of every single trick in the book. When finally I am off on an expedition, there is a certain satisfaction in knowing I have done everything I could have done beforehand. It is as if I attract all the eventualities in a positive way when I do my homework. The possibilities pursue me. Most problems have a solution; the positive surprises are the more common ones, and new possibilities are always arising. At other times I have been badly prepared. On those occasions it seems I am fighting a rearguard action the whole time. Before I have solved one problem, another has arisen. Then it feels as if bad luck is stalking me. In Britain there is an expression I have not encountered anywhere else—heroic failure. There is something stoic about striving that bit extra, in solving problems as each one arises. Behaving professionally is almost regarded as something negative. The manner in which one fails is decisive too; if it is done in the way a Brit considers stylish, an amateurish but heroic attempt characterized by courage and backbreaking toil may be greater than the goal itself. In a land like Norway things are different—either we succeed or we fail. To speak of style in connection with this is outlandish. Have we gone too far in Norway, simply calling failure "failure"? Perhaps not? I do not know. British polar explorers can be tougher than others, but when they fail it is almost always as a result of bad luck with the weather, their equipment, each other, or something else. It would seem now and again that bad luck persecutes them. And they are unlucky a fair amount of the time. These are not just my private observations; in Britain they are aware of this too.

After my expedition to the South Pole, for example, The Independent wrote: "This is a landscape you can try to master through strength (Scott, Shackleton, Fiennes) or intelligence (Amundsen, Kagge)." I do not believe it is first and foremost about ability, I think it is more about attitude. All the same, it is nice to be described as intelligent though I think this was the first time. When I was venturing into business I thought about things in a similar manner to when I set off on an expedition. I was humble in relation to the experience and knowledge of others and turned over as many stones as I could in search of answers. In the end I was left with a whole trail of contradictory conclusions concerning the starting and running of a publishing house. From then on I was reliant on myself to try to combine my personal shortcomings with a chunk of self-confidence so that I would be in a position to make good decisions. When making preparations I am often uncertain and at times afraid. Uncertain as to whether I am doing the right thing or if I am in over my head. The art is foreseeing what will happen. "Be wary then; best safety lies in fear," said Laertes to his sister Ophelia in Hamlet, when he was leaving her. I think that is good advice to give someone you love. If I grow too sure of myself, I become rather cocksure and not sufficiently self-critical. Then it is easy to overlook the small or not so small things that I should have noticed. All in all it is important to be a bit anxious—not only when making preparations—but until the goal is reached. As an outdoorsman I have in no way reached any final objective. I try all the time to take nothing for granted, and to sprinkle a moderate seasoning of worry into everyday activities.

The day I begin to think that everything is under control will be the day my outdoors life has at least one problem … me. The phrase "heroic failure" was dreamed up in Britain in the 1800s. Before that it was unknown, and to my knowledge the Brits have not exported it. So it remains quintessentially British. The background to it may be a romantic notion of the suffering hero. If you did not suffer, you were no hero, and the deed could be seen as nothing but a sham. These heroic failures thus had a moral dimension. After the race to the South Pole in 1911–12, it was more correct to use horses and motorized vehicles than dogs, even though the horses died on the way and motorized vehicles were unsuitable. Perhaps it was the British defeat at the hands of the Americans in 1812, and perhaps "The Charge of the Light Brigade" played a part in creating this idea of an apparently spectacular defeat being better than a "cheap" victory—or perhaps it was a combination of such events? The dream of the perfect defeat is still alive and well in Great Britain. There is something magnificent about such an attitude. Like Queen Victoria, however, I am no advocate of it. I would rather get there and get back home again. Preparations are all about foreseeing difficulties, but once I am underway with something or other, I do not worry about problematic situations until I actually encounter them. There is so much that can go wrong that it is just frustrating to worry about things beforehand. Besides, it is rare that something crops up that is anything to do with what I was worrying about. When a problem becomes an issue it is important to focus on the solution. Reality changes the whole time, as do the possibilities. It is all too easy (and exceptionally depressing) to consider the excuses and everything that might happen. For me, thinking positively is part of my preparation. I have a small but decisive bit of lore I actually think is completely self-taught; I have simply made up my mind not to think negatively about something once I am out there: "This is something I am going for. With heart and head, until it is proved undoable." This applies as much to big things as to small. There are plenty of good reasons for cursing once you have set off, but it can all too easily encourage a negative frame of mind. When we went to the North Pole, we agreed that swearing was not permitted—not on moral but on practical grounds. Swearing only pours fuel on a negative mood. In my journal from the expedition to the South Pole I wrote: "I have made up my mind to keep bad language to the absolute minimum. Just seems silly to go around swearing here." At home, of course, there is plenty of swearing and mouthing off at myself and others, but I try nonetheless to maintain this desire to manipulate myself into positive thinking and focusing on the solutions, when others might easily come to a standstill and be overwhelmed by the difficulties.

At times it might be somewhat artificial, but gradually it has become second nature to be positive—even though, once in a while, I do forget myself. It may seem as though we humans spend less time preparing for the truly vital decisions in life and more on the not so vital ones. When my girlfriend and I decided some years back to buy a place for ourselves, I was surprised at the way otherwise level-headed individuals started making an offer after being whisked once around the property. Buying a house is for most of us the biggest investment we will make in life, but I have the impression that only a few do anything but rely on that first impression, the estate agent and the prospectus. I often think it can be wise to rely on a first impression. At the same time I think it is not a bad idea to check and see whether there is damp in the basement. After moving in it is easy to spend more time on the house-warming party than there was time set aside to weigh up the house purchase. And the planning of a family holiday can easily take longer than the decision to start a family in the first place, not to mention possibly a former family.

On the other hand a good evaluation cannot be measured in time. That spontaneous gut response is often the best indication of the rightness of something. Of course it is not hard to imagine bad luck. All relevant airlines are on strike the day and following weeks you are supposed to leave; that I, on seemingly good grounds, still manage to come to a bad decision; that an apparently trustworthy individual breaks all our agreements and leaves us in the lurch, or that a storm gets up and does its worst week after week. My point is that often it is not about good or bad luck but rather about how I myself have acted beforehand and about what I do once underway. Difficult situations are always going to arise—that is statistically proven. The question is what I do before they hit. And how I react when they do. So the most important thing on an adventure is to be well prepared.

To get up in the morning at the right time is an adventures greatest challenge today, as much as it ever was. So when I am asked what the hardest thing is out there in the wilderness, I am never in any doubt as to my answer. There is something unspeakably tempting about remaining in one's sleeping bag when it is fifty below, as it was at times on our way to the North Pole. It beats crawling out of that sleeping bag and freezing as though one was in Dante's Ninth Circle of the Inferno, where chosen victims stand frozen up to their chins in ice. To save on weight we had neither sufficient fuel to warm up the tent nor extra underwear, so for the 63 days the expedition lasted I did not undress a single time. On that journey there was no shortage of reasons to remain in a sleeping bag: cold, wild weather, illness, tiredness, and injury. "There are certainly plenty who envy me, but few who would have swapped places with me," I noted in my journal on the way to the South Pole. The doubtful pleasure of lying in my sleeping bag and dreading getting up is reminiscent of the plot in a classic Alfred Hitchcock horror film. There is no tension in the bang itself, only in the anticipation of it. Of course getting up can be painful, but what is even worse is lying there dreading doing so. Because the greatest danger is—as in a good horror film—putting things off.

And get up I must. It is simply a question of whether I put it off for five minutes or five hours. Getting out of one's sleeping bag is not just the greatest challenge while doing outdoors, it is also the most vital. Most things are easy thereafter. All I may be dreading—frostbite, blisters or exhaustion—are, as a rule, never so bad once I get going. Often it is actually the other way round: when the challenge is met, these things grow less significant. Besides, no dream will be fulfilled if I go on sleeping. I do not know just how many times I have lain in a tent or a boat listening to wild weather outside, dreading getting up and creeping out. It took many years before I ceased to be surprised that it was seldom as windy outside as it sounded when I was lying in my sleeping bag, listening to the wind tugging at the flysheet of the tent or in the rigging. On expeditions, as in life generally, the final step is dependent on the first and vice versa. As an office worker and a father of small children, it has struck me that the greatest challenge remains the same. It is about getting up at the right time, regardless of where I may be and what I did the evening before. I know many who live differently and there is nothing wrong with that. Quite the opposite, in fact. It is not easy combining it with family life and also having ambitions at the office. Nonetheless, I changed from being a late sleeper to an early riser as demands on myself increased. What I know of discipline, I learned doing outdoors. If it is cold, it is tempting to put off the repair of the binding of one of your skis. When suddenly the wind gets up during the night at sea it is easier to stay lying there than going out and taking in sail, and if I am very hungry it is all too easy to nibble a bit of tomorrow's ration. But there are few problems that disappear of their own accord. At home it is perhaps not so earth-shattering if I stay in bed or put off making an unpleasant telephone call. But out there I suffer immediate consequences when I try to fool myself. For these reasons, I am in no doubt that my experiences in the great outdoors have made me far more disciplined at home. Besides, the day is made all the better once the unpleasant things have been got out of the way.

Roald Amundsen, the first man to reach the South Pole, wrote in his account that it was on the very days when the grounds for staying in the sleeping bag were most persuasive that things went best—once they got going. I have to admit though—before I come across as a moralist—that I do not always follow my own rules for living. And that is a good thing too. Even though I know what is best in theory and practice, I have to admit that for all the world's wisdom, on a more common-sense alternative, I am still to be found in my bed now and again, or putting off tasks. It is exactly this freedom to make "bad" choices that renders life enjoyable and challenging. And if I did not have a nine-to-five job and full-time children, I would still most likely be worried about getting up, though not necessarily in the morning. Our first daughter had colic. I had barely heard the word colic before and had no idea that it was possible for a baby to cry for such a length of time. On expeditions and at sea I generally get up at specific times. Suddenly, with baby Nor, I had to get up at all hours of the night and trail back and forth through the living room with her. It was an unbelievably tiring time for my girlfriend and me, but with hindsight I think of that period as one of closeness to my daughter and as one of the most intense and richest experiences of my life. Not because I have already forgotten just how hard it was, but because I know that I would not be without those sleepless nights now, in spite of all the hardship.

To Find Your Own North Pole

There were always people standing on the beach to greet legendary discoverers like Christopher Columbus, Captain Cook, Ferdinand Magellan, and Leif Eriksson when they "discovered" new places. These classic journeys of discovery—more accurately journeys of rediscovery, as most such journeys actually are—have to do with traveling as far as possible from where you start. Across, beyond, and perhaps above. To uncover something that can be described as a white spot on the map. The good news is that a small adventure contains many of the same elements and eventually experiences as any big expedition. The joy to be found in making the decision to reach for something beyond oneself enriches not only one's own life but the lives of those we care for. I do not recommend you to do what I have done, even though I know that it may be within your power. My heartfelt hope is that this book will help you—irrespective of your age or gender—to find your own North Poles. If that happens, it will make me happy. The outdoors is close. You can surprise yourself and experience something exciting no matter where, no matter when. It is not first and foremost about reaching a goal and being able to talk about it afterwards. It is about the journey and achieving the goals one has set oneself. A quiet evening away from home, a day in the forest, a weekend in the mountains, or sailing with friends can be the start of a very special journey. Perhaps we can

think differently, go a new way (perhaps even a shortcut), break with tradition, allow new feelings to express themselves, or risk a little more. Take me for example:

I have spent a good deal of my time living a macho life and on the outside seem like a tough guy. I barely know a soul who, entirely of his own choosing, has struggled and felt the cold quite as much as I have. If years ago someone had told me that one day I would be enjoying brief hikes with my kids and sitting on the floor playing with Barbie dolls—and enjoying that too—I would not have understood what they were talking about. Today I even have my own favorite Barbie dolls. And who knows, one day I might even come to like Ken or Blaine too. When some time back I drove several miles to buy a Barbie plane, I was just as pleased with the purchase as my daughters were. The long trips have also thought me to appreciate the smaller adventures in the outdoors more. The stillness in the wilderness is more profound and can be heard and felt more clearly than almost all other sounds. At home there is always a radio on, a phone ringing, or a car passing by. All in all there are so many sounds that I barely hear them. In the Antarctic, when there was not a wind, the stillness was far more powerful than back home. In my journal for day 26 I wrote: "Here stillness is all-absorbing. I feel and hear it. In this endless landscape everything seems eternal and without limit. The soundless space does not feel threatening or terrifying but comforting." At home I barely notice what is happening around me, but down there I became so drawn into my environment, so much a part of it, that stillness became part of me, something I could listen to. If I had enough energy for it, I made new discoveries each day. I was isolated from everything that at any given moment lay beyond my horizon, so it was only my nearest surroundings I could relate to. As the weeks passed, those impressions became stronger and stronger. Gradually I worked up a dialogue with my surroundings, a dialogue that was dependent on what I could contribute and what I was able to take in. Not a conversation in the normal sense of the word, but an exchange nonetheless where I sent out thoughts and was given ideas in return. Towards the end of the journey, on New Year's Eve, I wrote in my journal: "At the same time as I have felt my own smallness in relation to the natural environment, I have also felt an inner greatness. I have gone through terror and joy, known relief and disappointment, beauty and pain, questions and some answers, sensed closeness to the elements, given of myself and received, had the joy of physical exertion, and been strengthened in the view that there are still challenges and dreams worth giving one's all for. Although the great truths have not been revealed, I can understand that a time in the desert was decisively important for great leaders like Jesus and Buddha. Here one may experience what one cannot elsewhere." When I think back it is that closeness to the natural environment which made the greatest impression over those 50 days and nights I was alone in the Antarctic on my way to the South Pole. At times culture and nature can be contradictory but not on a journey such as this. My imaginings and my language were good tools for binding me closer to that natural environment rather than distancing

me from it. I became a part of the ice, the snow, and the wind in the course of that journey, and that environment gradually became part of me. Until then, most of my life had revolved around valuing the big moments, not those considered small. In Antarctica I learned that less can be more. I had to travel a long way before I realized this, while the Swedish songwriter Wille Crafoord understood it without having to travel so far south: "Little tastes a lot, less tastes best/a morsel in the mouth, so you're always wanting more." Perhaps it was rather late in the day to finally get the hang of that at the age of 30. I remember as a child how a small piece of chocolate tasted better than a big bit, but I never drew any conclusions from that. Each new piece tasted less good than the one before, and if I ate enough I felt sick. That is what economists call the law of diminishing returns.

Next time it was possible to eat chocolate or cake I again ate as much I could stuff down, naturally. But at times when there were only a few sweets, it meant I sat enjoying them. The character at the conclusion of Crafoord's song also has problems remembering the art of moderation. Now and then I still think it can be good to go the whole hog and dig in—but I am glad I have become aware of the pleasure of enjoying small helpings. It still lives with and I am reminded about this fact whenever I spend time in the outdoors.

When Heading Away from Civilization, I Certainly Do Not Miss All the Alternatives

Architects, of course, made this discovery long ago. "Less is more" is a motto and principle credited to the German architect Mies van der Rohe. This is a tad unfair, considering all the time the expression was familiar in architectural circles in Germany before he picked it up. And while we are on the subject, it was not Mies—as he is known to aficionados—who began to use the phrase "God is in the details." Mies was, however, one of those who really applied the consequences of this philosophy and in so doing became one of the ground-breaking powers in modern architecture. He followed his beliefs and showed that more of a good thing in architecture—as in an adventure—does not necessarily reap the most rewards. What is functional and beautiful in an object should be revealed by the omission of certain elements. Its strength as a whole will be increased by using less of something. In architecture it is not always relevant to talk about the law of diminishing returns. One tiny little excess there really can ruin the work. In the Antarctic I had the freedom to choose what I wanted at any time, as much as at home. But unlike life at home there were only a few restricting alternatives from which to choose. When I was not on skis, I tried to do at least two things at the same time. To repair equipment while I melted ice and snow, to read while I was eating, and so forth. By and large all these duties were routine and on the list. In addition I expended energy solving problems and challenges I had not encountered beforehand. There was nothing more to choose between or think about.

All in all I was very efficient on the ice and got done all I had to in the course of the day. At home I value having the most possible choices at any given time and being available almost all the time. To answer the phone, read e-mails, bring up the kids, prepare food, evaluate projects, make decisions on my own account and on behalf of others—all more or less at the same time. The more I am involved, the more I feel I am getting out of life. From a logical viewpoint I can not see that that is a bad conclusion. The problem is that at times it can appear limiting to have many tasks at the same time, and much to choose from. It is lovely to think of being faced with a choice of five different jams at breakfast, but it can also feel like an overload and therefore wasteful. When heading away from civilization, I certainly do not miss all the alternatives; there I simply eat good and healthy food, and the more time passes, the better it tastes. I do not see it as a goal to live as simply as this at home, but nor do I believe that the best thing for me is the maximum freedom of choice possible. I need the outdoors to remember this. To be faced with a plethora of options can be compared to having no choice whatsoever. I feel, at any rate, that the likelihood of arriving at a solution that works for me diminishes when the alternatives grow fewer, and when they become too numerous (because it feels impossible for me to investigate all the pros and cons of what is on offer). Both situations can render me powerless. If I have nothing to choose from I become frustrated, but if I make a wrong choice I do not just end up frustrated, I also end up regretting it.

Some years ago I read the book about Paris Hilton, Confessions of an Heiress, about her ultra-rich life as one of the heirs to the hotel chain of the same name. Hilton is, like an increasing number of people, famous first and foremost for being famous. I took note of a number of things, among them her way of travelling—utterly different to my own. "You must always pack more than you need—three times as much—then you use none of it and buy everything new." One of the benefits of packing so much, according to Hilton, is the way you are taken seriously in hotel lobbies. And if you are going to get to know a place then shopping is the best way to do it. In addition, what matters most is not where you travel, according to Hilton, but how. The best possible way is, of course, to travel with a billionaire chum in their jet, if you do not have one of your own. In the event of having to make do with flying first-class, Hilton advises taking your own food rather than eating onboard, something she loathes. The book is reminiscent of the French film La Grande Bouffe (1973). There the four main male characters take their success a little further on a weekend outing and eat themselves into the ground. Confessions of an Heiress is first and foremost amusing and well-written; it also has a serious side, because it reminds me of something I can all too easily forget: in a whole host of countries today over-abundance causes more social problems than do shortages. By this I mean obesity, traffic congestion, social unrest and the rat-race for status. Where I to have to choose between being frustrated by over-consumption or by hunger, I would naturally opt for a life like Hilton's, but so far that has not been necessary. I have three

daughters and I do not rule out the fact that Hilton may be a more significant role model for them than me when it comes to travel and seeking out the greatest range of options. For instance, I cannot see my girls being terribly impressed by my actions, when on the eighth day of my journey to the South Pole I discovered that the oatmeal soup tasted rancid. I was afraid of getting ill and had to throw it away. In my journal I recorded: "I look down on the snow in front of me. The soup has filtered through the snow. The grains of oatmeal and the raisins are lying on top. Have not the heart to let the raisins just lie there. I take off my right glove and pick them up, one by one. It is cold and laborious work. Stuff them into my mouth. Get my glove on. A bit of the sweet taste is left—I relish it." I remember that taste even now, and how those raisins felt in my mouth, and I am in no doubt that they were the best I have ever tasted. Strictly speaking, I see no reason at all for my children to experience the same thing. Perhaps they will read this book, but even if they do, they will need to experience things in their own way. All the same, it is my hope that they will not end up believing that life is so easy, or that too much of what is good is the way it should be. If they should ask me how they can balance the great and the small helpings in life, and outdoors vs urban life, I will not have an inexhaustible supply of answers for them. I wonder about it myself and am tempted by both. The perfect equilibrium is perhaps one of the most difficult things to find.

Now and again I dream about life on the ice, not just as a romantic or naïve notion, but because I am in no doubt whatsoever that life out there in all its simplicity was uncommonly rich. I felt I had everything I needed and that I was the richest man in the whole world, even though I never thought about what I would wear the next day—purely and simply because I had neither extra underwear nor extra outer garments. In a way I think I experienced something of the same feeling my five-year-old daughter Solveig did at Christmas. In the evening she was able to declare that she had absolutely everything she could ever want in life. And she concluded she had no need of future birthdays or Christmas celebrations. After several weeks, of course, she was already dreaming of her next birthday. It can feel both unpleasant and somewhat risky to change your own world, experience nature and spend less time in civilization. But perhaps it is even more risky to do nothing. Even more risky not to try to discover your own North Poles and experience how good life can be away from town, both for yourself and for those you care about. What you will regret in times to come are the chances you did not take, the initiative you did not show, what you did not do. If you say it is impossible and I say it is possible, we are probably both right.

Erling Kagge (born in 1963) is one of the world's most acclaimed polar explorers. In 1990, he and Børge Ousland became the first men ever to reach the North Pole unsupported. In 1993, he was the first person to walk alone to the South Pole. Kagge is also the first ever to accomplish the "three pole challenge," reaching the North Pole, the South Pole, and the summit of Mount Everest.

Kilian Schönberger

Andrew Groves

David Boyson Cooper

Photographer David Boyson Cooper draws viewers into nature's breath-taking landscapes, imbued with a free spirit and love for the outdoors sometimes revealed in candid moments of his friends along for these forays into the wilderness. Now based in Glasgow, he spent his formative years surrounded by the untamed sea and unspoiled environment of Scotland's Shetland Islands.

HIKING

"Do not follow where the path may lead. Go instead where there is no path and leave a trail."

Ralph Waldo Emerson

Sergio Jensen

As a travel destination, Norway is unforgettable for its breathtaking landscape of mountains and glaciers, waterfalls, and fjords. This did not escape the radar of London-based freelance photographer Sergio Jensen, who had just completed work at a voluntary environmental camp in Italy and was looking for an outdoor adventure with some friends. Starting in Oslo, the friends hitchhiked for two weeks through the country, living outdoors and, with the exception of one night in a camping lodge, sleeping under the open sky. Stopping in small towns and villages, they made their way through Odda, then Lillehammer and Nordfjord. "The way we chose our route was pretty random," Jensen recounted.

"I remember when we were deciding where to go on our first day, outside the airport in Oslo, a ladybird landed on our unfolded map and started crawling upwards pretty much along the highway, so we said we'll go that way. Made a sign for that town, went to the road and stuck our thumbs out. Our first ride was a police car, believe it or not."

Yamatomichi

The last thing you want to do is worry about the load on your back when out commuting with nature. As avid hikers and proponents of the ultralight hiking movement in Japan, Akira and Yumiko Natsume know this first hand. In 2011, they launched Yamatomichi, an outdoor gear brand focusing on the production of lightweight backpacks and related essentials for mountain-goers. Their Yamatomichi blog publishes news of their excursions and recommendations on trails, gear, efficient packing, food, and more. Starting in 2014, they plan to open up their shop to international customers.

Matt Pensworth

A transplant from the American southeast, Portland resident Matt Pensworth enjoys and documents the many outdoor activities that are so easy to do in and around the west coast city. From hiking and camping to skateboarding and snowboarding, the poetic and intimate moments he shares show that there is much life to be enjoyed in the out-of-doors.

Filson

For over a century, Seattle-based company Filson has been outfitting men in wool, flannel, and leather apparel made to withstand outdoor pursuits from gold-digging to logging, hunting, and fishing. As the outdoor aesthetic has gained in appeal among urbanites, Filson has widened its selection to accommodate them without alienating its existing customer base. The classic "Alaska fit" is looser with more room for active movement and layering. Meanwhile, many of the company's traditional designs are now offered in the new "Seattle fit," combining rugged materials with a slimmer, more tailored cut. Made of sturdy twill, wool, and bridle leather, the Filson range of luggage has a bag for every activity, from fishing and hiking to urban commutes.

Tree Tents

From conservation research to relaxing, forests should be used for more than just harvesting timber, believes Jason Thawley, which is why he came up with the Tree Tent, a spherical treehouse that offers year-round, above-ground shelter for up to two adults. Three meters in diameter, the cocoon-like structure is formed from hybrid aluminum and steam-bent green ash wood, spanned with a cotton canvas skin. Wool thermal liners provide insulation in cooler temperatures while wood stove, water, and electric options offer extra comfort.

With wooden floor and bunks, a weight of 120 kg, and roughly a day needed for assembly and rigging, the Tree Tent is not for the spontaneous camper. Still, it is designed for easy transport and on-site assembly with minimal, non-permanent impact on its environment. To make his idea a reality, Thawley, founder of the U.K. design and manufacturing studio Luminair, joined forces with his friends Duncan Ritchie, an expert in lightweight engineering, and Alasdair Ritchie, a hot air-balloon and airship engineer.

Scout Seattle

In a market that long prioritized performance and absolute functionality as the sole criteria for judging camping gear, Scout Seattle is one of the companies changing the stakes. Founder and designer Ben Masters adds iconic beauty and sublime design aesthetics to the equation. From the selvedge denim and Japanese chambray Field Bed to the Sunforger canvas Single Pole Tent held up by a collapsible hickory and antique brass pole, Scout Seattle appeals to today's outdoor enthusiasts who want to go back to the basics in style.

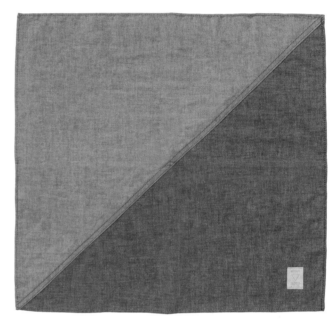
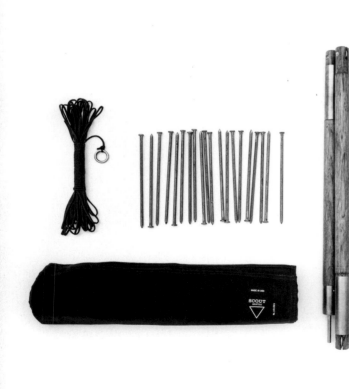

Hatchet+Bear

"Start where you are, do what you can, and use what you have." Ej Osborne took that motto to heart after abandoning the concrete jungle of London for the sylvan tranquility of Frome, Somerset. As Hatchet+Bear, Osborne uses simple tools and traditional methods on locally and sustainably foraged wood to create handcrafted utensils and bowls designed for everyday adventures. "I like to take over-processed products, turn back time, and take them on a different route," explains the product designer, bowl turner, and spoon carver.

Each bespoke creation reveals the holistic approach taken by its maker: transforming wood into strong, organically ergonomic products that make the most of the natural grain and curves, becoming more beautiful with age and use.

Furni Creations

What do we really need to survive? How about a backpack, a pocketknife, some sturdy moccasins, a battery powered LED lantern, and, to keep yourself busy, a DIY Bluetooth speaker set. Offering this and more, the Be Prepared collection by Furni Creations balances the fine line between bare essentials and limited edition luxury, bringing the heritage of the Canadian outback into the twenty-first century.

Furni is run as a one-man operation by Mike Giles, focusing on bespoke individuality through short-run collaborative design items, united in their clean, simple aesthetic.

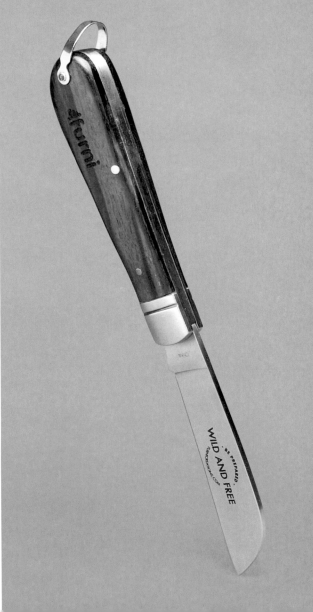

43

Topo Designs

Informed by the experience of its two founders as fishers, hunters, ski instructors, hikers, climbers, bikers, and travelers, Topo Designs creates outdoor bags, apparel, and accessories whose blend of functionality and style work equally well on weekend hikes as they do in the multitasking bustle of everyday urban existence. Both raised in the American West, co-founders Jedd Rose and Mark Hansen launched their first bag in 2008, drawing their design impulses from vintage French ski gear and Americana-inspired Japanese day packs. Driven by a shared sense of connectedness and calm experiences in nature, they eschew high-tech gadgetry made in Third World sweatshops. Instead they focus on high-quality, minimalist functionality, produced in their LEED-certified building in Denver, Colorado.

Topo Designs x Howler Bros.

Gone fishing? Topo Designs teamed up with Howler Brothers Austin, Texas to create the perfect bag for anglers. Founded by Chase Heard and Andy Stepanian in 2010, Howler Brothers crafts limited run clothing and goods that draw inspiration from the style and tradition of sports such as surfing, fly-fishing, and paddling.

Bjørn Rune Lie

Nature never seems to be too far away for Bristol-based illustrator Bjørn Rune Lie. He creates idiosyncratic characters that are human or animal (or both). They frolic through nostalgic outdoor scenes culled from his childhood in his native Norway or meander through ornate foliage drawn in fantastical detail.

Tentsile

It is a given that we have much to learn from nature, which is what treehouse architect Alex Shirley-Smith and his partner Kirk Kirchev did in developing the Tentsile Stingray. The lightweight, portable tent draws inspiration from the tensile technology underlying spider webs. It uses three anchoring points to find a central position in space; the tighter the tension, the stronger and more stable it is. With only three tree straps, two poles, and a removable fly sheet, the waterproof polyester tent offers a surface area of 7.5 sqm and shelters up to four people. Depending on how high it is mounted, 10 to 30 minutes are needed for set-up and just a few minutes to dismantle. For those who do not mind a few rocks or roots driving into their backs at night, the Tentsile Stingray can also be pitched like a conventional tent in dry conditions.

This page, clockwise from left: Andrew Groves conducts a Woodland Woodcarving Workshop; Miscellaneous Adventures Whisky Cup; Secret Stash Pouch; workshop woodcarving kit consisting of an axe, carving knife, crook knife, folding saw, and woodworking apron.

Miscellaneous Adventures

There is nothing like being one with nature through honest, manual labor to counter our fast-paced world inundated with digital images and information overload. Parallel to a successful career as an illustrator working primarily on the computer, Andrew Groves found a way to unite his passion for the outdoors and his creativity more directly with his handicraft project, Miscellaneous Adventures. Inspired by a hiking trip to northern Sweden, where he discovered the traditional handicrafts of the Sami people, Groves now crafts and sells wooden utensils for use on outdoor adventures. Groves' illustrations are full of natural motifs and the English native has always tried to live an active outdoor life to fuel his creativity. Working out of his barn in West Sussex, Groves sources wood from the surrounding woodlands and handcrafts each unique piece using traditional techniques and a few essential tools: an axe for felling, a hatchet for hewing, a carving knife, and a gouging knife. He also shares his handicraft in woodland woodcarving workshops, empowering urbanites to return to nature.

Sitka

A multitool that honors the adventure of life on the road, the Hobo Knife by Canadian lifestyle brand Sitka in collaboration with Case XX is a useful addition to any survival pack and is beautiful to both hold and regard. The tool folds out and then splits open into knife, spoon, and fork—the latter with integrated bottle opener. Custom hobo-esque etchings on the blade and a Sitka-branded oak handle conjure up the nomadic spirit of the knife's namesake.

Sandqvist

The spirit of Nordic nature, with its vast unpopulated areas, soaring mountains, and remote cabins, meets urban city lifestyle in the bags and accessories by Swedish company Sandqvist. Its three founders grew up together in a village in central Sweden before they settled in Stockholm in the late 1990s. Reflecting the early devotion to outdoor life shared by the three owners, Sandqvist bags are uncomplicated and functional, made from carefully selected and durable materials with minutely worked details. A range of classic designs and tasteful colorways allow for a smooth stylistic transition from city to country and back again.

Robin Falck

For many, a weekend cabin in the woods is the perfect retreat from the distractions and obligations of the urban everyday, a place for rediscovering one's place in nature. With a year of compulsory military service rapidly approaching, young Finnish designer Robin Falck felt the urge to create a refuge of his own, quickly and efficiently. Once he found a small plot in the archipelago of Sippo located outside of Falck's native Helsinki, he had to move quickly. To bypass the bureaucracy of obtaining a building permit, he planned a cabin with extremely restrained dimensions: 96 sq ft (9 sqm). Using mostly recycled materials and locally sourced wood, Falck built the cabin in about two-and-a-half weeks, naming it "Nido" (Italian for "nest"). The design of the micro cabin maximizes the living space and natural light, welcoming in the beautiful surroundings.

I PRAY 4 WAVES
IN SAYULITA, MEX

Poler

Since it launched in 2010 in Portland, Oregon, Poler has quickly gained a following for its unpretentious and inclusive approach to high-quality gear and outerwear for action sports and the outdoor lifestyle, from skateboarders, snowboarders, surfers, and bicyclists to weekend campers and road trippers. Through social media and their #campvibes and #adventuremobile hashtags they share the stories and adventures of the communities they serve and are themselves a part of. An interview with co-founder and creative director Benji Wagner.

We know your work as a photographer; how did you become the mastermind behind an outdoor gear company?

I have wanted to start a brand for many years and was always thinking along those lines. We felt we came up with an original concept that was worth putting everything we had behind. We are grateful so many people have responded positively.

How would you describe your relationship to nature, to being outside?

I grew up with a father that was always encouraging me to do all kinds of outdoors stuff from hiking to riding bikes, to going on road trips and taking photos. It was very important to me and expanded my view of the world.

Are you a hiker, cyclist, ... How do you approach the outdoors?

I'm a skateboarder and snowboarder, a cyclist, and do all kinds of things outside. I am a father of three so that takes up most my time. I go on walks in the forest with my kids and try and get them out as much as I can.

What is particularly "Portland" about Poler?

Portland is one of the world's great cities. It is right in between the ocean and the mountains and is part of the glorious Pacific Northwest. There is an endless array of awesome things to do outside here. It also has some of the best, most creative people and is affordable. These are all things I see reflected in Poler.

You are a small company that launched in 2011 but you already have an extensive team of skateboarders, snowboarders and photographers who share their experiences via all sorts of social networks. How important are they for your brand?

Many of them are friends of ours and we appreciate their support immensely. Hopefully being a part of Poler has brought them some recognition and helped them as well as us. We have been overwhelmed by the positive vibes and support.

Poler is about having local adventures—is it important to have your products made locally too?

We make a variety of products all over the world. We try to make things affordable and of good quality. Some things are made in the USA, some are not. We have products made in many countries and will no doubt have many more.

What are your three most favorite Poler products these days and why?

I am really proud of our first line of jackets. We spent years developing them and have tried to bring together modern fit with classic aesthetics and technical functionality. Of course The Napsack will always be a favorite: it's unique, useful, and fun in so many ways. We are also very proud to have worked on a collection with Nike including shoes and apparel and will be continuing to work with them.

What outdoor adventure is still on your to do list?

There are too many to list. I have traveled a bit but the world is large and I have only scratched the surface. I would love to visit so many places. I recently went to Iceland for the first time and that was very cool.

What was your most beautiful and/or extreme outdoor experience?

I would say some of my favorite places are Southern Utah, the Oregon Coast, New Zealand, and Iceland. These are places that I could visit every year. But there are so many others. There is no limit!

Kate Sutton

A low-impact, non-invasive pastime for millions of people across the globe, birding establishes a sense of connectedness with nature. Perhaps that's why birds are one of Kate Sutton's favorite motifs. In charming detail she populates her whimsical illustrations with birds, trees, and other wildlife. "I am at my happiest in the countryside or by the sea so maybe this explains nature's influence in my work. I especially love to draw trees and birds; I find the patterns in nature fascinating," she says. The freelance illustrator and maker is based in the coastal town of Southport, England.

Cody Cobb

From brittle, pumice-covered slopes in Washington State, to the lush, rugged coastline of Kalalau Beach, Kauai in the Hawaiian archipelago, Seattle-based photographer Cody Cobb documents the beauty and power of the earth's surface and atmosphere in his ongoing photo series "Monuments." When he is not out roaming—often solo—the landscapes of the American West in search of seemingly untouched nature, Cobb works as a freelance motion designer and 3D animator.

Mike Seehagel

From the Canadian Rockies to the prairies, the photographs of Mike Seehagel have captured the essence and wild beauty of western Canada. The photographer and motion designer based in Calgary is part of Great North Collective, a community of photographers and artists inspired by the Canadian landscape, who are sharing their visual impressions with viewers around the world.

Tom Powell

Travelling through New Zealand, Canada and Australia, Tom Powell documents the landscapes and the people he encounters, living independently and off the beaten track. The English photographer and graphic designer shoots with a range of vintage cameras for the aesthetic qualities of the images, their durability when packed in a bag for traveling, and the conversations they begin.

Kammok

Based in Austin, Texas, outdoor company Kammok has had two main goals since its launch as a Kickstarter project in 2011: creating technically innovative and high quality outdoor lifestyle products and giving back to aid humanitarian crises around the world. The flagship product, the Roo hammock, is made from a proprietary ultra-lightweight, ripstop, and breathable fabric and is roomy enough for two. Founder Greg McEviley came up with the idea while considering bedding solutions to help people in malaria-stricken countries. This vision is continued through Kammok's commitment to donate 20% of its profits to humanitarian aid, including the nonprofit Malaria No More.

HIKING CHECKLIST

Preparation is essential for any outdoor adventure. Having the necessary supplies and equipment can make a difference in your overall enjoyment and experience.

1

3

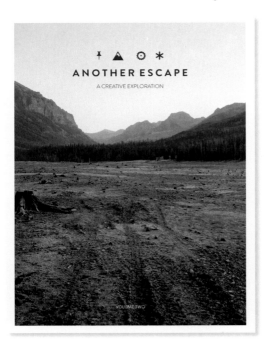

2

1. MEINDL: Bavarian shoemaker Meindl continues over 300 years of quality shoemaking with the evolution of its Island trekking boot, a perennial favorite since first being introduced in 1990. The newest iteration of the Meindl Island features an advanced MFS Memory Foam system that provides individualized comfort in wear.___ 2. CAMPFIRE COLOGNE: Trapped in the urban jungle but yearning for the forest? Light up some cedar sticks over your flannel shirt or beard to enjoy the smells of campfire memories.___3. ANOTHER ESCAPE: Draw inspiration from creativity lovingly presented in this biannual print publication introducing inquisitive, innovative people who are excited about the world around them.

1. SWAROVSKI: Crystal clear binoculars to discover the beauty of nature, the Swarovski Habicht offers state-of-the-art optical precision in traditional design, both lightweight and rugged. ___ 2. FILSON: Since 1914 Filson's Mackinaw wool Cruiser jacket has provided outdoorsmen with durable warmth and comfort. Perfect for layering in the classic Alaska fit or in the slimmer Seattle fit for a more versatile look. ___ 3. FILSON: Limited edition issue of the Filson Cruiser Shirt in 100 % virgin Yukon wool, patented in 1912 to meet the needs of outdoorsmen of the Pacific Northwest. Presented in a commemorative wooden box with a tin cloth envelope containing copies of the original patent documents. ___ 4. GRAYL: The Grayl Stainless-Steel Water Filtration Cup works like a coffee press to filter out bacteria, viruses and other impurities in 15–20 seconds. A replaceable filter or optional purifier lasts 300 uses to make 150 l of drinking water.

1. MISCELLANEOUS ADVENTURES Experience oneness with nature with every sip from this small whiskey cup, hand carved by English artist Andrew Groves in the style of the traditional Sami Kuska of Finland. Made from sustainably sourced wood and seasoned with linseed oil.___2. NALGENE For an even lighter pack, Nalgene halved the weight of its iconic wide mouth water bottle. The Ultralite HDPE Wide Mouth Bottle weighs just over 100 g and withstands temperatures from −100°C to 120°C___ 3. WAKAWAKA Lightweight, efficient, and socially responsible. Proceeds made from selling the WakaWaka solar-powered lamp with optional USB charger at competitive prices are used to make them available to developing communities at an affordable rate.___4. SKINTH Bushcrafter's buddy. Made from military tested Cordura, the Skinth Trailblazer keeps your tools quick at hand with seven pockets, a double stitched belt loop, and customization options.

1. OPINEL Foraging for mushrooms is a favorite pastime in France, so it is no wonder that French cutlery brand Opinel created a folding knife for just that. With a curved blade for harvesting, a serrated back for scraping, and a boar bristle brush for cleaning.___
2. TOPO DESIGNS The rugged Cordura base and water-resistant cloth upper, interior laptop sleeve, and tasteful color combinations make the Topo Designs Rover Pack ideal for adventures both urban and outback. ___3. SNOW PEAK The Snow Peak Titanium Colored Spork is a double weight saver. Not only does titanium make it light, you also have spoon and fork in a single utensil. Available in three vibrant colors achieved through non-paint electric ionization. ___4. SNOW PEAK INC. Stronger than steel and weighing next to nothing, the Snow Peak Titanium Single Wall Cup can be used for both drinking and cooking, and will not taste like the soup you had the night before.

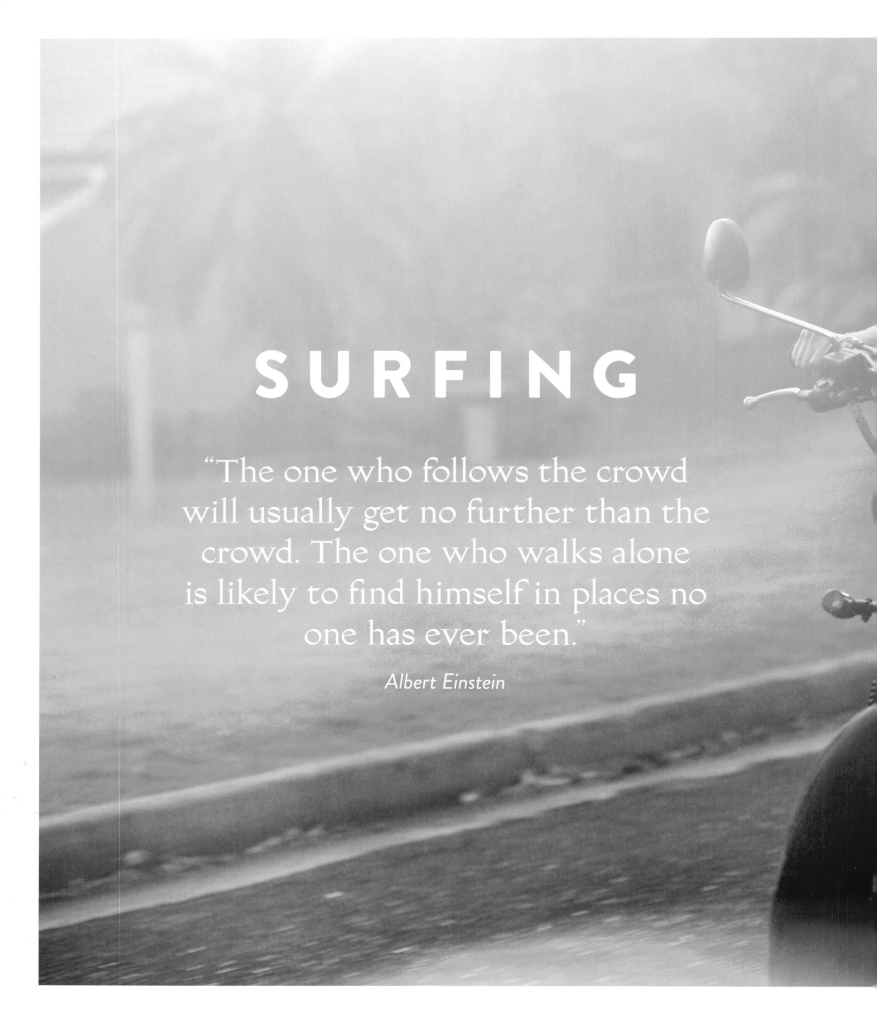

SURFING

"The one who follows the crowd will usually get no further than the crowd. The one who walks alone is likely to find himself in places no one has ever been."

Albert Einstein

Deus Ex Machina

Driftwood Surfboards

The magic of surfing lies in the harmony found with the waves and the wind. But for nearly half a century the production of polyurethane foam core surfboards has been all but kind to the environment and posed health risks for their makers. David Forsyth, founder of Driftwood Surfboards, is part of a new movement to make surfboards more sustainable. Since 2009, the Cornwall-based company has created hollow wooden surfboards from reclaimed and sustainably harvested wood, sourced as locally as possible. Each board is unique with its own history of where it is from and how it was made. As opposed to the millions of conventional surfboards that, once discarded, languish in landfills to release toxins into the soil, water, and air, Driftwood surfboards can be recycled or simply decay at the end of their life.

Rake Surfboards

Keiron Lewis

Based in the surf mecca of Noosa Heads, Australia, Rake Surfboards was started in 2009 by artist Adrian Knott to unite his passion for alternate surfboards and design. Today the surfboards are shaped by Knott and Andy Warhurst from their small workshop, integrating traditional methods of surfboard building with vibrant resin tints, pigments, and finishes. Knott's original artwork may be seen adorning the surfboards as well as the retro-inspired surf attire for the brand's clothing line.

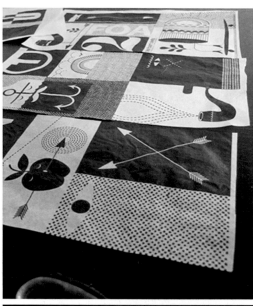

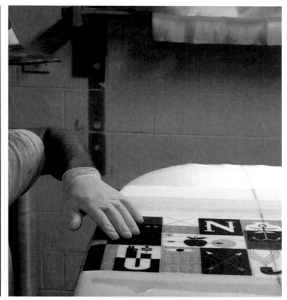

Chris Burkard

*Born and raised in the coastal town of Arroyo Grande, California, Chris Burkard
has served up some of the best surf photographs in recent history. The young photographer's
unique use of natural light and sense of composition contribute to a signature style and
approach that layers landscape photography and principles of photojournalism with surf and
other outdoor subjects. He is currently a senior staff photographer for Surfer Magazine and
freelances for various international publications.*

Images of water abound in your work. Have you always been drawn to water? What is your personal history with surfing?

Growing up near the coast, the ocean has always held a place in my heart. From a young age I have been captivated by it and engulfed in its power and beauty. Feeling the power of the ocean water up close and personal is a unique feeling. That's why I love bodysurfing and surfing. You are able to be a part of the ocean and experience its movement. Capturing images from the water is taking something I love to be a part of and documenting it, hoping to express this wonder and excitement for others to enjoy.

Why isn't it enough to simply experience the outdoors? Why photograph it? What drives you to step back from one to enjoy the other?

Traveling and experiencing the outdoors definitely inspires me. That's where my heart is: traveling and seeing the world. I don't travel to find myself. I travel to experience new things and share them with people. I enjoy bringing back photographs that I can share and that stir the emotions of the viewers that see them.

Aside from their stunning beauty, many of your surfing pictures are unconventional because of their setting, like Iceland or Kamchatka. As someone from sunny California, what is it about these extreme(-ly cold) places that draws you to them?

The backdrops and setups you get on those cold-water trips are like nothing I've ever seen. The beauty of cold-water surf is often the work that it takes to score waves that no one else is willing to surf. Most of my memories are all moments of pain or suffering while on these cold water trips. But these stories make a trip exciting to relive and scoring great waves or seeing beauty out in nature all is a bonus.

Images abound of surf scenes with beautiful bikinied bodies and sunsets. How do you break the stereotype? What do you go for in a shot, what is the story you look to tell?

I like to give people something they haven't seen before and often that's in the form of a cold, remote surf destination. It's the opposite of the comfortable tropical beach at sunset, and that's what I think I love about it so much. I try to take a pretty organic approach to my shots. I love it when things just unravel, but sometimes it is good to have some forethought for good images. I think it makes for a more fluid trip when you can picture in your head what you want to see and shoot before you do it. At the same time, if you get too premeditated then it's hard to just let things happen on their own sometimes. It's all about finding a balance. I can tell I scored a perfect shot when the moment tells a story or a moment of peak action aligns with your camera angle.

You've shot for a lot of surfer magazines. What are surfers looking for in these photos—(how) is that different from what the non-surfer sees?

Surfers can really understand what is happening in the image and get really picky with small things that non-surfers wouldn't notice. A surfer can look at an image and say "I doubt he made that air because his footing is off in the photo." So for a surf image to really come together everything pretty much has to be perfect ... the wave, the surfer on the wave, the composition, and the lighting all play equal roles in getting a usable magazine surf image.

What gear do you take with you no matter where you go?

In terms of camera gear I shoot with Sony NEX cameras, my Nikon D300s, a wide variety of lenses, and then my Aquatech waterhousing. When I'm off the beaten path Goal Zero makes a must-have line of solar charging products that keep my batteries and gear charged. I'm fortunate to be backed by some great companies that keep me dialed in for travel.

What about other outdoor sports—cycling, hiking, sailing ...?

I'm really drawn to hiking and camping. They are a pure way to experience the outdoors and I find myself day dreaming of trekking along long hike trails and setting up camp in the remote outdoors. I also do a bit of climbing and free weekends are often spent trying to plan trips to places like Yosemite or Joshua Tree.

What would be your dream outdoor photography assignment?

I think it would be pretty rad to do another bodysurf series. To travel around and take bodysurfing to some exotic places. It is such an undocumented form of wave riding and getting those unique water angles of bodysurfing would be fun to do.

What was your most frightening, dangerous, or extreme outdoor experience? Would you do it again?

I was in Chile and we had a drunk boat captain who was driving us next to this wave that we were shooting, and a big set came and he drove us right into the set, and the whole thing washed over the boat. All my camera gear was soaked, totally toasted, done, gone. It was a total nightmare. I'm lucky I didn't fly off the boat. I felt like I was at SeaWorld or something. And then in Russia, I got put into jail because of passport issues. My passport wasn't stamped correctly, and that was really gnarly. I got deported through Korea; that was

pretty crazy. I did a lot of praying in that moment! You go on a lot of trips and nothing goes wrong, and then something happens that really makes you appreciate where you live.

What is your favorite photograph of the outdoors?

My Chile shot that won the Red Bull illume in 2010. The shot is a prime example of my focus on incorporating dramatic landscapes into my photos. In my mind it's a beautiful moment where everything came together. I cherish that image in my career.

Please describe your most beautiful outdoor moment—that you did not manage to hold onto with a photograph.

I had the chance to climb the face of Half Dome and really didn't take any photos that entire climb. Being on the face of such an amazing peak is a surreal experience and slightly frightening, but looking back the images really could not have done that climb justice.

"Most of my memories are all moments of pain or suffering while on these cold water trips."

The Northern Post

Although having one's own outdoor adventures is the most fun of all, reading about them can also be rewarding as a source of inspiration and information. The Northern Post brings readers closer to the spirit of the frontier with a mix of interviews, apparel and gear reviews, personal essays, and photographs. Founder Dustin A. Beatty is a photographer, founding editor-in-chief of Anthem magazine, and principal owner of the social media, PR, and marketing agency, You Are Here.

Deus Ex Machina

Deus Ex Machina celebrates a spirit of creativity, individuality, and exploration born from a culture originating in the 1940s that embraces the motorcycle as the ultimate expression of applied art. Deus first opened in Sydney, Australia in 2006 as a combined showroom, café, and cultural venue, bolstered by an enthusiastic sense of community. Its spirit of inclusiveness and authenticity quickly extended to surf, skateboarding, and fixie culture as well. Deus has gone on to establish concept stores in locations where these cultures of fun and freedom are best lived out: in Canggu, Bali, Venice, California, and Milan, Italy.

Geoff McFetridge

Based in Los Angeles, California, Geoff McFetridge works creatively across the disciplines of graphic design, film, and visual art. He is known for a powerful visual style that explores the tension between geometric and organic forms, detail, and abstraction. His designs have been featured on album covers, snowboards, athletic shoes, wallpaper, and more. In addition to creating animations for his own short films and music videos, he also designed the opening sequences for films such as **The Virgin Suicides** *and* **Where the Wild Things Are.** *Born in Canada, he was schooled at the Alberta College of Art and the California Institute of the Arts.*

Nature and outdoor scenarios seem to feature prominently in your work. Would you call yourself an "outdoors person"? If yes, what is your way of spending time outdoors? What does it mean for you?

If being an "outdoors person" means doing things like surfing, trail running, riding bikes, skiing, and camping, then yes—I love that stuff. Even though I live in Los Angeles the outdoors is something I like to have as part of my everyday. I can't always sleep under the stars, but we bought our house to be close to the mountains and Griffith Park. I get to my studio through the park by running or riding over a small mountain. There are a lot of places near my house where I can do many, many miles without seeing people. There is true wilderness 30 minutes from my studio. I like the duality of that, and being in this city of so many millions. What does outside mean to me? This is a bit cheesy but—outdoors is my meditation. I don't think you get inspiration from meditation, but meditation leaves you open for inspiration.

How do nature and outdoor scenarios find their way into your work? Do they relate mostly to briefings or are they more a transformation of your own experiences?

I think I am a different person for the experiences I have had outdoors, and that is the main thing. Really I should spend more time in galleries and less time goofing off! I do some commercial work for some outdoors clients though, because I like what they do and I use their gear. In my work for Patagonia, for example, I like to think that I am working from within my own experiences. It is pretty common to find surfers who are also artists, but most ultra-runners, cyclists, or skiers are not artists, so I think it is interesting that I can interpret these worlds visually. Maybe that is unique. On a deeper level I am interested in worlds. Surfing, skiing, cycling, and trail running are worlds. I wonder sometimes if I purposely seek out worlds that are very uncreative, sort of mindless as a way for balancing out my life?

"We are all 'outside' but on a sliding scale of memorable-ness."

All the stuff I love the most is stuff where literally my mind is blank or at least active in a super pea-sized spot. And yet this pea-sized part of my brain can lead me to memorable experiences. Mostly I am alone, but sometimes sharing them with other people, but mainly pushing myself to my limits physically (and at times mentally). The feeling I get is that over the years I have learned how to "invent experience." With skateboarding I would often marvel how I was totally sweaty and eating crap down a flight of stairs while surrounded by people in suits going to work. Similar to when you get out of the water after surfing and someone might be just sitting on a towel eating snacks reading a book. We are all "outside" but on a sliding scale of memorable-ness.

111

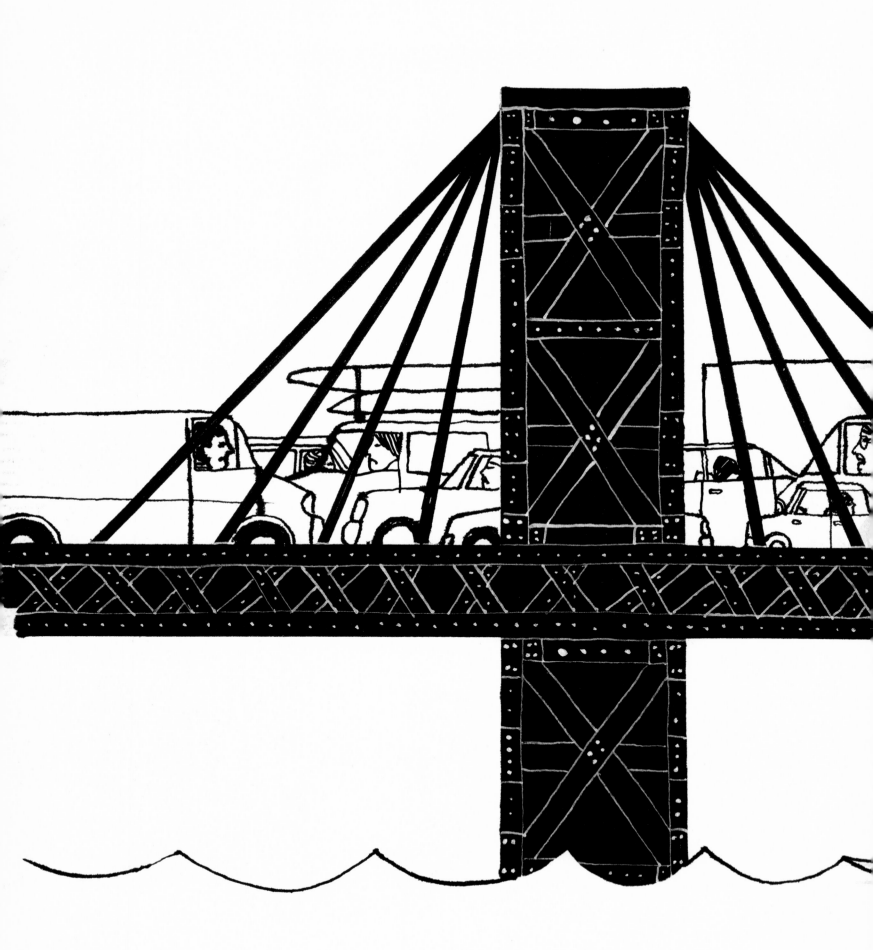

Do you ever go outdoors to draw? Could you describe your process?

My wife and I have two daughters and we take a camping trip across the U.S. every summer. We spend around two weeks each way camping and driving small roads. I always have work that pops up so I do a lot of work on picnic tables or in our van. When we get to Evanston, Illinois, where we spend the summer, my studio is on the back porch. So I draw through rainstorms and intense Midwest heat.

This book is all about being outside in nature, but its title also opens up the notion of being an "outsider." How do you reconcile being at the cutting edge with having widespread commercial success?

I have always felt that the world has always responded best to my best work ... but that is my perspective. Ten years ago I made the change to really look inward for my inspiration. It lets the work develop in a way that is sort of automatically deaf to anything that comes from it. I feel my best work is my most personal work and so—can success come from being an outsider? Approached as a practice, can outsiderness become critical to success?

What was your most beautiful moment in nature?

Silently chasing a little fox through a forest in waist-deep powder in the backcountry of Hokkaido, Japan last winter.

What was your most extreme outdoor experience?

Well, where I grew up it was really cold. As a kid I lived in St. Albert in Alberta, Canada. I was playing in the snow once and my ear turned black and the doctors said I would lose it. All the skin kept peeling off and falling onto the floor. But I didn't lose it.

What outdoor adventure is still on your to do list?

Ski in Alaska.

Your ideal outdoor meal and setting?

I love to ski in the resort with my kids. I like to pack my backpack with food and get my daughters (ages 10 and 5) to take off their skis and walk into the woods. There we set up a picnic on a log with hot chocolate, Nutella on tortillas, sandwiches, whatever. It's super simple food, but the key is to remind them that we are in this amazing place, and that it might seem normal with the lifts and people, etc. but really we are way, way deep into the mountains and we have magic shoes (skis) that make it possible to be there.

What pieces of outdoorsy gear do you never leave your house without?

I don't often use it in the summer in California—but pretty much any other place or time I take my Patagonia Houdini jacket with me. For layering, wind, sun, cold protection. It packs into the size of a power bar but is lighter.

What words of wisdom would you give the outdoor aspirant?

I am a big fan of the door-to-door. Do stuff that you can do right from your house. An hour in the car is easy to do in Los Angeles. For me that means a three-hour trail run instead of driving to the beach for a one-hour surf. So the surfing happens less often for me lately.

Emil Kozak

Blue sky, white clouds, the angularity of raw wood and stone tempered and shaped by pounding waves—graphic designer Emil Kozak drew inspiration from Spain's west coast in developing "Sea You Soon," a capsule collection of t-shirts and sweatshirts for Spanish eco-friendly surf brand TwoThirds. Born and raised on a small island in Denmark, the call of the ocean has never been too distant for Kozak: "Whenever I get a chance to get out of the city, the power of the roaring sea and the endless horizon, and the big, majestic clouds overwhelm me with inspiration and, somewhat, fulfillment." Now based in Barcelona, he often collaborates with the skateboarding and surfing scenes, whose passionate, independent, and improvisational spirit continue to strongly influence his creative output.

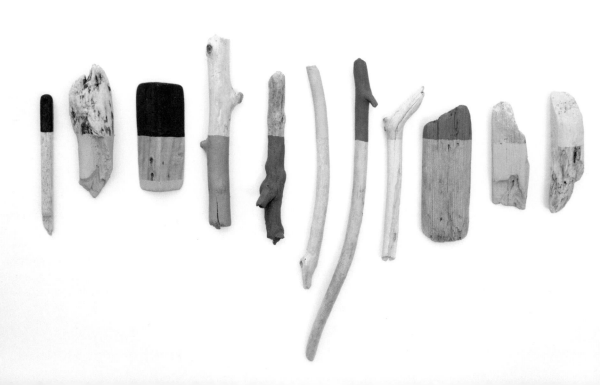

Indoek

All things creative and inspiring related to waveriding culture are celebrated by "surf-centric" blog and brand Indoek. Founded by filmmaker and photographer Drew Innis and designer Matt Titone, also a co-founder of the creative studio ITAL/C, Indoek highlights the heroes of surfing and their stories, and collaborates with like-minded designers on limited-run accessories.

Offering instant intimacy and a touch of romance for beach basecamps or even a backyard barbecue, Indoek's Wave Wam Teepee (in collaboration with Stefan Wigand) is a portable refuge for two to three adults (or the equivalent in children and dogs), made from cotton canvas supported by collapsible bamboo and aluminum poles.

Style-savvy waveriders will appreciate the artfully handcarved Indoek Wax Kit (in collaboration with Todd St. John), while the Indoek x WaveWam Teepee offers a romantic beachside retreat.

Mollusk

Since 2005, when it opened its doors just a few blocks away from Ocean Beach in San Francisco, followed by a second shop in Venice Beach, Los Angeles, Mollusk Surf Shop has become an institution among surfers and artists living in these beachside communities. Nurturing an aura that goes beyond your ordinary surf shop, Mollusk offers itself as a creative space that integrates surfing, art, craft, music, film, and visual media. Its offering of hand-shaped surfboards and locally-produced apparel and crafts is complemented by art shows and music events which contribute to the intimate, eclectic atmosphere.

Neon

Flattering, fashionable, and functional, Neon makes wearing—and designing—wetsuits fun. It all began several years ago when English surfer Elsie Pinniger, frustrated with the lack of choice for women at the time, decided to design a wetsuit of her own. Her suit attracted compliments and Pinniger went on to create more designs and perfect her wetsuit sewing skills with a leading wetsuit manufacturer. Thanks to growing demand for her bespoke creations, what began as a hobby evolved into a business. Under the brand name Neon Pinniger now offers a range of stylish made-to-order wetsuits for women and men produced locally in Newquay, Cornwall, the epicenter of surfing in the UK. The Neon website allows you to customize your own wetsuit, picking from 11 colors and 15 stylish designs.

Hydroflex

No surfer likes a broken board, and Hydroflex Surfboards has come up with a solution to avoid the problem altogether. The secret lies in a patented 3D lamination technology developed by German innovator and shaper Rouven "Bufo" Brauers. This process roots epoxy resin and fiberglass into the surfboard's foam core, making it incredibly light, responsive, and resistant to pressure dings and delamination. The 3D glassing technology is used for all Hydroflex boards, which are produced locally in Oceanside, California. Of particular note is the unique SuperCharger construction, which can be pumped with air to adjust the internal pressure for customizable flex. Higher pressure means a stiffer board for increased speed, while lower pressure dampens the ride in a choppy surf.

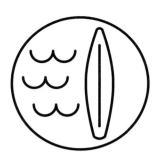

SURFING CHECKLIST

1

1. DEUS EX MACHINA: Your custom motorcycle, surfboard, or fixie by Deus ex Machina will be imbued with the carefree spirit that has made the Australian brand such a success in Sydney, Los Angeles, Milan, and on Bali. Pictured here, the Deus Drover's Dog Custom is perfect for catching the surf with verve: with a Yamaha SR400 at its heart, a surfboard rack, and vintage Firestone Deluxe Champion tires.

1. STEVE HARRINGTON: Los Angeles-based artist Steven Harrington let his imagination run wild to create a surfboard engraving for the Greenroom surf culture festival in Yokohama. The project initiated by The Critical Slide Society, a surf brand from Australia, commissioned Harrington and four other artists to design a traditional wooden Hawaiian alaia surfboard shaped and hand-cut by renowned Australian shapers Paul and Sage Joske of Valla Surfboards. ___ 2. NEON: Tired of neoprene in black and gray? Pick your style and color combination online from Neon's one- and two-piece warm-weather neoprene suits for women and men. ___ 3. SHWOOD FOR PENDLETON: Tradition meets innovation. Oregon's legendary Pendleton and newcomer Shwood teamed up for these limited edition wooden sunglasses. With laser-engraved signature Pendleton patterns and a matching Pendleton wool storage pouch.

1

2

1. FOLCH STUDIO Witness the sublime beauty and spirit of surfing in the inaugural issue of Eldorado, the new print magazine by Barcelona-based designers, Folch Studio.___2. DRIFTWOOD Driftwood's new CNC Chambered Surfboard in Paulownia timber exchanges the fishbone frame often used for hollow wood surfboards with a chambered structure achieved through computer numerically controlled (CNC) techniques to reduce overall weight as well as labor hours. This model features a silk laminated inlay designed by Beccy Jayne Taylor.

1. NEON: Stylish but warm. When the wind feels fresh, the long-sleeved crop top by Neon features fasten-free design for comfort and flexibility. Made from 2 mm limestone-based neoprene.___2. MOLLUSK: The Pennant Trunks by cult Californian surf shop Mollusk facilitate a smooth transition from surfboarding to beach combing. Made from a comfortable cotton-nylon blend with a classic drawstring closure.___3. INDOEK: There's no surfing without wax on your board, and Indoek collaborated with Todd St. John to create a beautiful and functional wax kit case, whose unique design is reminiscent of surfboard shaping planes. Comb tines are on the bottom edge, while the detachable lid doubles as a scraper.___4. DANNY HESS X HOWLER BROTHERS: Bodysurfers do not need a surfboard, but the use of well-crafted handplanes can help control your ride on the wave. In his San Francisco woodshop, master shaper and woodworker Danny Hess handcarved these limited edition handplanes for Howler Brothers from locally sourced and salvaged wood.

CYCLING

"For my part, I travel not to go
anywhere, but to go.
I travel for travel's sake.
The great affair is to move."

Robert Louis Stevenson

While Out Riding

While for some, cycling is a pastime, for others it is a calling. Thanks to the expanding landscape of blogs dedicated to two-wheeled adventures, we are able to share in their passion and fuel our own. At his blog While Out Riding, cycling enthusiast Cass Gilbert has shared with readers beauty seen and lessons learned from his many bikepacking expeditions around the world. While the blog has only been around since 2009, Gilbert's biking history is much older. An avid traveller since his late teens, he started off hitchhiking and exploring the bus routes through Latin America. But the moment he discovered bicycle touring, "there was no turning back."

From the start, sharing his experiences from the road with photographs and words has played a major role in his adventures. One of his early treks in the late 1990s was an epic two-year, 25,000 km tour from Sydney, Australia to London, England to raise over £23,000 for the Children with AIDS charity. Outfitted through sponsors with, at the time, state-of-the-art technology, he was able to write travel articles and email posts for the tour's website from the road—a practice that was still relatively new at the time. Gilbert went on to ride through Central Asia by tandem bike, through Tunisia and Morocco, around southwest China, Laos, and Cambodia. He also co-ran a bike touring business for several years in the Indian Himalayas. In recent years, he has turned his attention to exploring the backroads of North and South America.

It was during a bike journey from Alaska through the American backcountry that the dedicated blog While Out Riding was born, growing since into a more comprehensive website with gear reviews, packlists, Q&As, a photo gallery, route notes, and even recipes for hungry cyclists.

Thanks to his engaging and informative writing and compelling photographs from the road, Gilbert has funded his travels as a freelance journalist for the likes of Cycling Plus, What Mountain Bike, Singletrack, Mountain Flyer, Adventure Cycling, Boneshaker, Cycle, and wired.co.uk.

Joe Cruz

If you are looking for inspiration or advice for your next cycling expedition, Joe Cruz's blog Pedaling in Place might just come in handy. Posts range from how best to carry your gear on a touring bike to comments on bikes, trails, beauty, and hardships of bikepacking through the Andes. The writer and professor of philosophy and cognitive science has toured and raced bikes all over the world, in the Americas, Europe, the Middle East, and Asia.

Berlin 2 Shanghai

For their 30th birthday, twins Hansen and Paul Hoepner decided to embark on the journey of a lifetime: a six-month, 13,600 km bike tour from Berlin, Germany to Shanghai, China. They successfully raised over € 9,000 through crowdfunding, won a few sponsors and completed their trip, along with multimedia documentation that has now been transformed from a travel blog into a film and a book. In between book readings, Hansen Hoepner reflected on the roots and ramifications of their remarkable voyage.

While the Berlin—Shanghai route was certainly the longest bike tour you have made, it was not the first. What inspired you to first try out long distance bike touring, and what made you do it again and again?

I have always loved bicycles. In 2003, I travelled alone through Cambodia and Thailand by bike. The first tour we did together was in April 2008 from Maastricht to Milan. I wanted to visit the furniture fair and couldn't afford a plane or train ticket. I convinced my brother to come along. Covering about 1,000 km we made our way to Milan on 37 kg, full-suspension bicycles that we built ourselves—we named the bike the Great Hannemann. Thanks to our poor equipment and freezing weather (snow in the Alps) we arrived after the fair had already closed down. But that was no longer important: we had tasted adventure and life in the outdoors, and we wanted more. After that we tried to do one long bicycle tour every year. You get to know people and places in a different way. You can travel pretty fast and don't have to worry about gasoline or perfect roads. The feeling of conquering long distances with your own power is amazing.

How did your love affair with bicycles and cycling begin?

I studied product design in Maastricht and specialized in bicycles. I built my own bike frames and built my own bikes. Paul has also always been a lover of the outdoors and so we discovered our love for this combination of bicycle and nature. The bicycle's simple technology (when compared to that of a car or other motorized vehicles) has always been an inspiration. And the freedom to go wherever you want, to decide for yourself, to be independent.

How far do you cycle on average per day or per week in your everyday life, compared to when you go on an excursion?

Normally we ride between 5 and 10 km a day; on a tour around 100 km a day. But it's different on a tour because you don't have much else to do other than ride!

Of course we are curious: travelling for so long on bike you needed to pack for various climates and conditions, but without being overloaded. What did you take with you? What things turned out to be unnecessary, what things were surprisingly helpful?

Equipment is always a question of money and the countries you ride through. You definitely need a very good bicycle (ours were from Tout-Terrain, extremely reliable and highly recommended); a warm sleeping bag and a light silk sleeping bag; and a four-seasons tent, so you can have a good home in the desert as well as in the cold mountains. A large bush-knife also proved to be quite useful: it's great for hacking wood and comes in handy for repairs and such. Clothing according to the onion principle let's you combine as the climate requires: a thin waterproof jacket, a warm fleece, and functional underwear. Good shoes are indispensible, as wet shoes can be uncomfortable and even dangerous.

You also need a good navigation system. Our iPhone3 and iPhone4 were extremely practical. It's also good to have a solar power supply, since pedal power generators don't make enough electricity for a camera and telephone/navigation system. What ended up being unnecessary was food with high water content (too heavy); dried food saved both weight and energy. Using universal instead of multiple charging units also saves in weight. Our rule of thumb was that it's better to take too much, and then to get rid of it along the way. But we were pretty good at not having too much that was unnecessary.

> "Our rule of thumb was that it's better to take too much, and then to get rid of it along the way."

Is there anything you wish you had taken with you but didn't?

Yes! For example an open mosquito net for sleeping under. Sometimes it was too hot for the tent but there were too many mosquitos to sleep outdoors. That can rob you of sleep, which is extremely important on such a tour. Also, our saddlebags weren't good. You shouldn't cut corners with that—Ortlieb is the best. Another thing we should have brought were little German souvenirs to thank our hosts. This could be anything from sweets and coins to pens and non-prescription medicine. In some countries we could have made a lot of people happy with things like that.

A Polaroid camera and film would have been great for taking pictures with people and giving them a copy straight away as a thank-you gift. Some people really appreciate that.

We also missed having a good Leatherman. We had a cheap imitation, which turned out to be an annoyance more than anything else.

We also could have benefitted from a kind of "magic letter" translated into all the languages of the countries we rode through, which in an emergency could explain who we are, what we were doing, and where we were going. Trying to explain yourself without knowing the language can be exhausting.

And finally: more time.

You financed a huge part of your trip through crowdfunding, promising various souvenirs and postcards in exchange. Would you use this model again? What do you think about asking others to fund your adventures? What do they gain from it?

We asked people to help support our project, which was not just an adventure, but foremost a book project. We could never have gotten a cent for just going on a trip. There's no harm in asking. We have also supported various projects. It's a choice one makes. Crowdfunding is great. It enables anyone to realize their project if they are willing to invest a lot of promoting and convincing. It makes the world more independent of credit, banks, and loan sharks. We would do it again, but eventually with more souvenirs and less projects promised to do along the way. The latter became more of a burden than we thought. When you support crowdfunding, it is mostly ideal value you get in return. You have to know for yourself what you can do with that. Another advantage is that when you give others money, you'll be supported in your own projects. I think I will give back to crowdfunding as much as I receive. You can see it as a kind of community that makes money available when money is needed. And it gives you a good feeling. Personally I really enjoy giving and helping others, even if I don't receive something tangible in exchange. And maybe that is the essence of this way of financing projects.

What was your most beautiful moment during your trip?

At 2,550 m near the Himalayas. That was geographically and emotionally the absolute highlight of the trip. Untouched nature, incredible landscape, it was a breathtaking feeling after riding for nearly 10,000 km to arrive at this wonderful landscape, far from civilization. At the highest point there stood a Tibetan prayer flag on a mast, flapping loudly in the wind. The snow from the nearby peak was swirled through the air by the icy wind in minute, sparkling crystals like magic glitter. And the high we got from lack of oxygen at that altitude topped it off.

The most frightening?

When we were in Kazakhstan and attacked by three Kazaks because we didn't want to drink vodka with them. They forced us off the street and started beating up on us because we had refused their invitation. We had no idea how far they would go, if they wanted to kill us or merely teach us a lesson—that was the worst part. By chance a truck

driver saw us and stopped, and chased them off with a crowbar while we fled. For a while I thought the tour would end then and there—I was afraid it could happen again and then worse. Our equipment was damaged but everything could more or less be repaired. And they didn't steal a thing. And after that, nothing of the sort ever happened again.

What is the most important piece of advice you have for someone planning to do a first long-distance bicycle excursion?

Nearly anyone can undertake such a bicycle trip. Whether or not you succeed is not about the equipment, but rather the willpower and time. If you are willing to give up all comforts and understand that you will encounter many difficult situations, then you can make it. What you get in return is a feeling of immense freedom. Still, you should never be too proud to break off a trip if it just doesn't work anymore. Our health is our prime asset, and we always have to protect and nurture that, come what may.

Traveling long distances can be so meditative; the journey is the goal. When you're at home in your everyday lives in Berlin how do you find a similar sense of calm and harmony?

I dream of new tours and imagine the craziest things that could happen along the way. Daydreaming is one of my main hobbies. And if the travel bug hits me too strongly, I do a little bike tour. It doesn't have to be more than 50 km, but enough so that I can feel the freedom. That rebalances me.

How would you describe your connection to nature?

We have always been very close to nature. Our parents always took us on adventures and taught us to respect nature. During our trip, we never left our trash behind. Even when we had to schlepp it along for weeks before we could dispose of it properly. This and other principles give me a sense of security when I am in nature. It's the law of reciprocity: "I respect you and you respect me."

Now that it's over—the trip, the book, the film—where to next?

One dream has been fulfilled, now we need another. We don't have any concrete plans yet, but we would love to do the Pan-American Highway from the Tierra del Fuego in Argentina to Alaska.

151

Tal Roberts

Tal Roberts

Jones Bikes

For some, a full-suspension bike is the most comfortable for tackling rugged terrain. Others prefer a hardtail bike to truly feel the ground on which one rides. Oregon-based framebuilder Jeff Jones has gained a following for his rigid titanium and steel bikes, whose ideal combination of shape, material, fork, and handlebars offers high performance with natural suspension. His signature 3D SpaceFrame and trussed fork are built to absorb shocks while maintaining control. His patented H-bar handlebars allow for a more upright riding position for comfort and handling. Jones also offers the same geometry in a traditional diamond frame in titanium or steel and in various configurations. All orders are individually considered with the customer to assess their needs and preferences.

CYCLING CHECKLIST

1. RAPHA: The centerpiece of the capsule collection developed by Graeme Raeburn, product designer at UK cycle-centric brand Rapha, with his brother, English fashion designer Christopher Raeburn, is the Rapha & Raeburn Hooded Wind Jacket. The packable city riding jacket is made from reappropriated military parachute canopies. Made in England by outerwear manufacturer Cooper & Stollbrand.

1

2

3

1. ORTLIEB: Ortlieb was founded in 1982 in Germany following the viral success of the panniers and handlebar bags that young Hartmut Ortlieb started sewing in his mother's garage after getting soaked on a rainy bike trip just a year before. 30 years later, Ortlieb continues to be loved by cyclists for its wide range of rugged, well-conceived bags and bicycle mounting system. ___2. URSA MAJOR: Perfect for men freshening up on the go, the bamboo fiber Essential Face Wipes by Vermont-based Ursa Major are infused in an aromatic tonic with notes of cedar, citrus, lavender, rosemary, and vetiver. Comes in a carton with 20 individually wrapped wipes. ___3. WANDERLUST: Japanese outdoor brand Wanderlust creates bags from high-tech Cuben fiber for all your ultralight adventure needs. The slender Wanderlust Cutlery Zip Pod is durable, flexible, lightweight, and waterproof, offering quick access to clean chopsticks, spork, or small tools.

1

2

3

1. SCRUBBA: Caught off-grid with dirty laundry? The Scrubba wash bag is a pocket-sized washing machine with integrated scrub board that lets you wash your laundry in a matter of minutes. Australian inventor Ash Newland came up with the idea when he was packing for a trip to Mt. Kilimanjaro and realized he had little space for extra clothes. ___ 2. WANDERLUST: The Wanderlust Cuben Rounded Bags in translucent black or white keep your cookware intact and separate from the rest of your pack. Custom sizes can also be ordered directly on the Wanderlust website. ___ 3. VAPUR: When space as well as weight matters, the collapsible, reusable Anti-Bottle by California-based Vapur might just do the trick. The Vapur Eclipse in matte olive holds 0.7l of hot or cold beverage and comes with a widemouth flip top SuperCap for one-handed access.

1

2

3

4

1. GIRO: One for all. The Surface Multi-Sport Helmet by California-based Giro offers protection with understated style. The In-Form fit system allows you to adjust the helmet with the turn of a dial. ___ 2. SAWYER: The Sawyer Squeeze Filter System is a lightweight and simple solution for clean drinking water on the road. Fill one of the included pouches with water, screw on the PointONE filter and squeeze the bag to purify the water while it pours into your water bottle or directly into your mouth. Sawyer claims that its 0.1-micron filter will remove 99.99999 % of all bacteria and protozoa, and purify 1 million gallons of water (enough to last a lifetime). ___ 3. JONES BIKES: Jeff Jones reinterprets the classic diamond frame for his limited edition Titanium Diamond Frame. Pictured here with the Jones Ti Truss fork, which is lighter and stiffer than a conventional fork, offering good tire clearance for a fat front tire. ___ 4. BOKER: The Boeker family has created highest quality gear since 1829, when it produced its first sabers in Germany. Today alongside its high quality blades and with a slight spelling change in its name, Boker also produces tactical gear that fuses modern materials with innovative design. Watertight with a sturdy grip, the Boker Plus FC-3 LED Flashlight is a reliable companion no matter what your adventure.

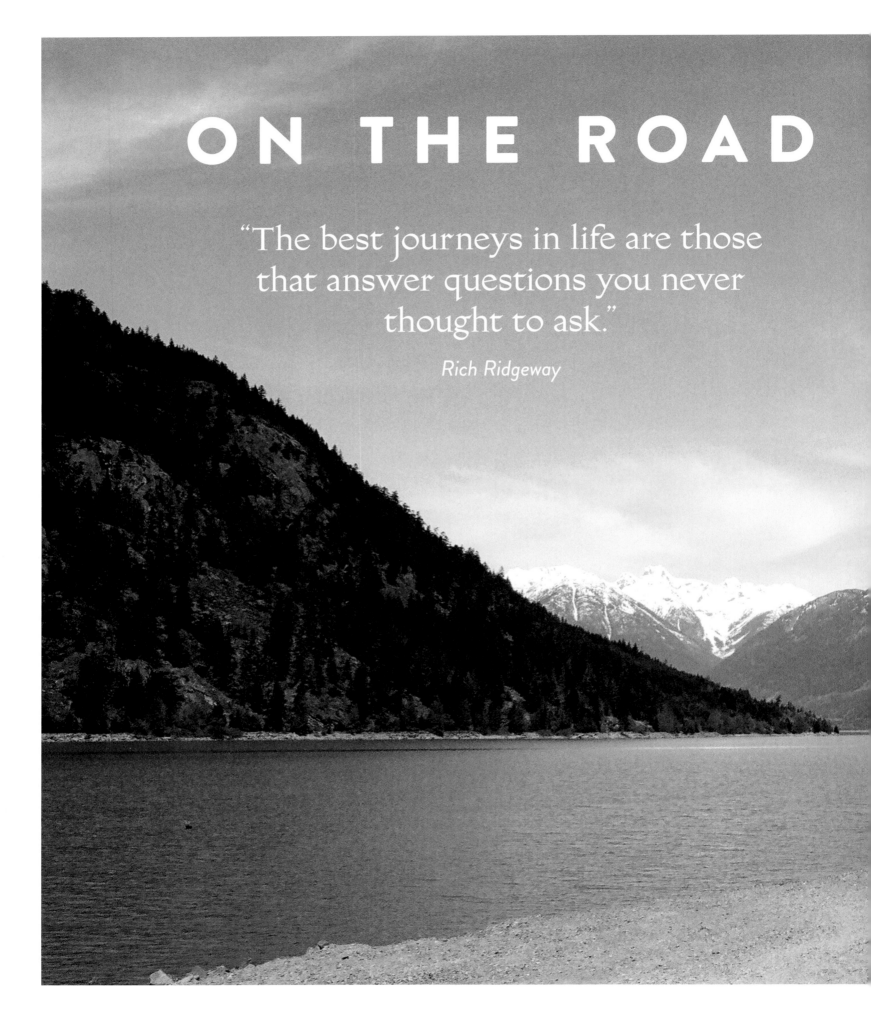

ON THE ROAD

"The best journeys in life are those that answer questions you never thought to ask."

Rich Ridgeway

Our Open Road

In 2012, Adam and Emily Harteau answered the call of the open road by embarking on a road trip from Los Angeles, California to Tierra del Fuego, Argentina and back, with their one-year-old daughter Colette. But what started off as a one-year tour in their in their VW Westfalia has turned into a way of life. Having visited some 12 countries to date, they are now into their second year of travelling overland through the Americas. Since the beginning, they have documented their overland travels with writings and photographs on their blog Our Open Road and across social media platforms, offering an ongoing "modern family portrait" that has won the hearts of some 60,000 Instagram followers today.

You've referred to your trip as a chance to reexamine the American Dream. After over a year of being on the road, what does the American Dream mean to you exactly?

The American Dream—work a good 9 to 5 job, get married, buy a house, have 2.5 kids, buy a bigger & better car, work longer to get a promotion, save your money to retire so you can then enjoy your life—is an ideal that has no value to us. Instead we choose to live for each day, follow our passions, live simply so our lives may be rich, listen to our deep selves and tune out the clamoring of modern static. Our American Dream is to embrace the spirit of American pioneers, thinking on our feet to stay on the road, opening ourselves to the endless possibilities of exploration.

Can you tell us a bit about the backstory to your trip? What inspired the trip? Why the Americas and not Asia or Africa, for example?

We have previously traveled in and about four continents together—Africa, Asia, North America, and Australasia. When Emily was pregnant with Colette, Adam was working on an art-film project that would have put us in India and Nepal when Colette was between 4 and 10 months old. When that fell through, we knew it was time to plan our next grand adventure. Driving the Americas was a logical and exciting proposition, as we had not been to South America and our first day out we would be in a foreign country with our home on wheels. Logistically, it is the easiest decision as crossing borders is fairly direct, we can communicate easily as Emily speaks Spanish, the cost of living is very affordable, and there is so much culture and stunning beauty to be seen.

How did you prepare for the trip—had you ever done a road trip of the sort before?

We had done a 14,000 mile road trip around the U.S. and Canada, overland trips in Zambia, Botswana, Namibia, and South Africa by way of bus, rented 4 × 4 truck, private plane, and hitchhiking—so we knew to keep our hearts and eyes open, be flexible, and to expect the unexpected. However, a trip of this magnitude—and with a toddler—required excel spreadsheets, brainstorming sessions, garage sales, packing and repacking, and endless lists and revisions. Adam spent a great deal of time modifying the van—researching and installing a new refrigerator, custom designing and building Colette's front seat, a complete engine swap from 95hp VW to 135hp Subaru, researching and installing an interior LED lighting system, and designing and installing a security system for the van including welded exterior window bars, a lock-in-place front window system, and exterior padlocks.

What are some of the challenges you have faced as a family travelling with a small child, and how have you addressed these?

We see traveling as a family as a great benefit, not a challenge. Officials and locals alike warm to us as foreigners in a way that is vastly different than our experiences traveling without a child. The stern officer's tough face suddenly softens as he sees Colette sleeping peacefully in the back of the van; a rural family that we may view us as rich gringos, suddenly views us as parents and our common ground brings us into the folds of their community in a very simple way as our kids play together.

How are you plugged-in to the Internet?

Out in the wilds we mostly free-camp and have no need or want for this modern trapping. In towns we usually stay at campgrounds that have WiFi, which we connect to eagerly with our laptops and cellphones to stay in touch with family and friends, conduct business, and share our experiences with the greater world through our blog www.ouropenroad.com and on Instagram.

We suppose if there were a downside to overlanding, you wouldn't be doing it for so long—can you imagine ever settling down in one place?

Even when we lived in Los Angeles, we were gone nearly every weekend camping, hiking and exploring our great state of California, so "settling down" was never part of our vocabulary. Perhaps one day we will again live in a house that isn't on wheels, but for now: home is on the road.

What does an average day of traveling look like for you? Do you have a set amount of driving time vs. rest time? How do you choose where to go and where to stay?

The wonderful thing about life on the road is that there is no average day. We explore when we are in fascinating areas, we move on when things are dull. We choose our route based on many factors including guidebooks, our own Internet research, recommendations from fellow travelers we meet, and the most valuable: local knowledge.

What outdoor activities do you make a point of doing as much as possible?

Adam is an avid surfer, so if there are waves, he is on them; Emily makes time for yoga and the occasional run. We hike as a family often.

What are the top ten essential things that you have in your camper van?

- good attitude
- camera and lenses
- laptop
- ATM card
- insulated aluminum water bottles with flip-top straw
- pressure cooker
- mini Cuisinart
- hanging fruit basket
- tools for the van
- spare parts

Can you explain the concept behind your 24-Hour Bazaar?

When in towns with an abundance of artisans, we curate a fair-trade market featuring whatever goods inspire us. This may include rugs, blankets, clothing, and hats for men, women, and children, jewelry, ceramics, home wares, antique textiles, bags and decorative arts. This catalog of offerings is for sale for a limited time—often just 24 hours—hence the name "24-Hour Bazaar." Shipped directly from the field to your doorstep.

What have been some of your favorite places you've visited during your trip and why?

This could fill a book all on its own! Baja Mexico was a wonderful intro to life on the road—the solitude and rugged beauty coupled with great waves left a lasting mark on our memory. The food, arts, and culture of Oaxaca are incomparable. Costa Rica's well-preserved biodiversity of floral and fauna are unrivaled in our travels thus far. Colombia is populated by the friendliest, most welcoming people. Peru has a rich, beautiful artisan culture and a breadth of ecosystems that astound.

Your van was recently broken into and robbed. Was that an isolated incident? How do you feel about that?

We are super bummed that we got robbed and our personal space was violated, but are grateful that after 14 months of traveling this is the first incident of consequence to report. Theft is an unfortunate part of modern life in most places worldwide.

You are currently in Peru. Dare we ask: where to next?

As we write this, we are in transit to Chile. Our visa is up, so onward we go!

Between the two of you you've seen a lot of the world, even before this most recent undertaking. What is the most beautiful place on earth?

The next destination ...

Campa

If plans for your upcoming road adventure do not include sacrificing all the comforts of home, the Campa ATT (all terrain trailer) is one of the more compact, rugged, and complete solutions around. The trailer measures about 3.3 × 1.8 m with a dry weight of 860 kg. A veritable "Swiss army knife" of trailers, the stainless steel construction comes with ample storage, a raised sleeping platform that fits various pop-up tent configurations, and a built-in kitchen fully equipped to serve up to six people. Optional customizations include a hot water shower system, a water purification system, solar panels, and additional power generators.

Wilderness Collective

Have you ever wanted an adventure but were not sure how to organize it, let alone fit it into your schedule? The Wilderness Collective might just have the answer. Since 2012, they have has been hosting outdoor excursions for men, aimed to have maximum impact in a short period of time. Group adventure packages include weekend off-road motorcycling through California's magnificent Sequoia groves, horseback riding in the Sierra Nevada, and snowmobiling along the legendary Iditarod dogsled trail in Alaska— each complete with equipment, catering, and camaraderie. Founder Steve Dubbeldam, a native Canadian based in Los Angeles, sees the Wilderness Collective as creating "a context for people to grow, whether it's personally or in relationships or even push themselves physically to do things that are scary for them, things that are hard for them."

West America

Portland-based motorcycle maker James Crowe and his longtime friend and bicycle builder Jordan Hufnagel decided they needed a break from daily life, and a big one at that: a motorcycle odyssey from British Colombia, Canada to Patagonia and back. To fund their trip, they launched the project West America in 2012, producing camping gear and other handmade outdoor paraphernalia for sale as well as their own use. Since then and even more so after starting their actual road trip in August 2013, they have shared their experiences via social media, giving voice to their pioneering spirit, and building a fan base that counts in the thousands. During a quiet moment in Mexico, James Crowe shared his thoughts on their ambitious undertaking.

How did you come to building and riding motorcycles?

When I was 19 I had just finished tech school and was working in a high-end hot rod shop in Portland, Oregon. I had never owned a motorcycle at that point, but was learning the realities of not living at home and having unlimited space to store and work on car projects. Also the time and cost involved in putting together a nice vintage car is very high. I decided to sell my 1926 Model T Ford project along with my 1958 Chevy and bought a basket case Yamaha XS 650. At the time, I was living in my van so it was something I could leave at work and stay late to work on. By the next summer I was on the road and have been hooked since. My interest in the styles of bikes has changed since that first build but the feeling of escape is the same.

What about bicycles? You're sharing this amazing experience with Jordan, a custom bicycle builder. But motorcycles and bicycles pose such different approaches to transportation and experiencing the world. What's your take on human-powered transport?

Bicycles have been a huge part of my life since I was able to walk. My dad raced mountain bikes in the early 1980s, and I followed in his footsteps growing up. We would spend all summer travelling around Canada, racing every weekend. I stopped racing full time when I was 16, but bicycles are still a big part of my life. The experience is very different from motos, and staying active is very important to me.

What is the appeal of travelling long distance by motorcycle, as opposed to bicycle or the camper van (that we saw you posted on Instagram), for example?

I enjoy all forms of travel and they all have a place in my life depending on the goal of the trip. When you do long trips on the motorcycles you are exposed to everything. You can't change the temperature or turn off the rain; you're stuck with it. I love the vulnerability you are exposed to on the bike. Plus, motorcycles have taken me places no car could go. I have experienced the best days of my life on my motorcycle. You can camp anywhere, hide the bike, sneak it around gates, lift it over things—the possibilities are limitless.

What are you riding? Thanks to your excellent motorcycle building skills we assume your bikes have been perfectly tuned to your needs.

Ha ha! I wish they were perfectly tuned. This build has offered me many new challenges, and building bikes that will do over 30,000 miles with plenty of dirt is going to be a test. We started with mid 90s Honda XR600s and only made modifications to improve travel distance, reliability, and storage capacity. So far after 5,000 miles we have made a couple of changes, mostly to suspension to compensate for the load of the luggage in heavy off-road riding. The way we pack the bikes and move things around will be a constant evolution, and I can definitely think of a couple things I would do differently in the future.

You two decided to take an epic trip—but you also prepared for it, creating a brand and a blog behind it. What was the motivation behind making your personal adventure more public?

We have both been hugely inspired by others and the fact that they shared their journeys with the public. People thrive and prosper through storytelling and the lessons learned in them. It's an incredible privilege to be able to share our stories with others and hope that they might find an aid in their journey through them. With the blog we have a section that is devoted to being a resource guide for others who are thinking of doing a similar trip, and we get a chance to showcase our photography that we are both very passionate about.

"When you do long trips on the motorcycles you are exposed to everything. You can't change the temperature or turn off the rain; you're stuck with it. I love the vulnerability you are exposed to on the bike."

You've had an opportunity to produce a capsule collection of outdoor apparel with Woolrich. What was the concept behind that and what's your favorite from the collection?

The opportunity to work with Woolrich has been amazing. The team they have working there now is full of energy and is steering the company back in the right direction. The concept for the project was for us to help them design a small USA-made line of gear that we would produce for our trip to South America. It all had to be practical and wearable on and off the bikes. So far, the Westamerica x Woolrich Jacket has proven to be the most used and weathered piece. We have thrown everything at it from snow in the high cascades of Oregon to 90-degree sand in Baja.

Travelling for such a long time means not only having new adventures but also leaving a lot behind. What have you had to give up to take off?

The great thing about the trip is that it was meant to be a transition point in our lives. To leave the old behind and start anew when we return. Attempt to improve the way we were living our lives and fix the problems that we faced. Somehow, during our trip prep, we both fell into amazing relationships with two very special ladies. They knew of the trip

the whole time and are very supportive, but it will still be tough being away for so long. Luckily, we have some plans for them join us on parts of the trip.

So the nerdy part: what are the top 10 most useful equipment items or accessories that you have with you in your pack?

These are the things that get used every day on the road: sleeping bag, multi-fuel stove, duct tape, Leatherman, clean socks, toilet paper, journal, Spanish dictionary, Nikon FM2, lighter.

Is there anything in terms of gear, accessories or clothes you wish you had packed but didn't?

I must say that I have become very fond of Jordan's Teva sandals now that it is getting hot, and all I have are hiking boots to wear. Otherwise we have a good kit and can't carry anything but the essentials.

Where are you sleeping most nights? In what, on what?

We camp every night. Depending on the weather it might be in a tent, hammock, or under the stars. We usually try to plan where we want to end up, and once there, look for a good spot to set up. When we are in big cities we usually end up in a hostel for a shower and to do some laundry.

Are you plugged in at all via smart phones or GPS, or just hitting the Internet cafes where you can?

We are pretty low-tech. Usually we just wait till we are in a city to hammer out a bunch of Internet work. We have a little laptop and an old iPhone that was given to me without any cell service to check emails.

What are some of the off-bike outdoorsy things you and Jordan are doing during your trip—have there been any highlights?

We both love getting off the bikes. We can't bring much with us, so traveling activities usually involve finding amazing swimming holes and remote areas to hike into. Once we are in Central America we hope to post up at a good surf spot for a bit and enjoy the ocean.

What has been your most extreme or dangerous encounter so far?

Riding through northern Baja has given us plenty of sketchy moments. The dirt roads are not maintained to any standard, and before we got down there, Baja had just gone through its rainy season. You can be riding what looks like a good road, and then out of nowhere it disappears into a huge sand wash. The first couple of days we hit a couple going way too fast, and it felt like we used up our free cards pretty quickly. We have learned to respect the terrain and the feeling of being accountable for all your actions. Not depending on signs or markers has made the experience very real.

The most beautiful moment?

It's still so early in the trip, but a couple unforgettable moments have been waking up above the clouds in Big Sur and blasting through the cactus forests of northern Baja at sunset.

What has been your favorite place so far during the trip and why?

I am writing this on the ferry from La Paz to the mainland of Mexico, and all I can say is that we will definitely be spending more time in Baja with our bikes unloaded of all the camping gear in the future.

Witness Company

"The spirit of the Great Plains, endless prairies, Rocky Mountains, muddy waters, dark hollers, and open highways" find expression in the handcrafted biker jewelry by Brooklyn, New York jewelry studio Witness Company. Using the traditional technique of lost-wax casting, founder and artisan William Bryan Purcell hand carves each creation in wax and then casts it in solid brass or silver. His knuckledusters, pendants, and bracelets draw on Americana iconography to convey an ethos of brotherhood, authenticity, and strength.

El Solitario

Like the landscape where they are created, El Solitario of Galicia, Spain makes custom motorcycles that are rugged and beautiful—a compelling mix of old and new with a fierce, if not punk, spirit of individuality. Founded in 2008 by David Borras and Valeria Libano, El Solitario has gained international recognition for their unique aesthetic and dedication in creating their one-off vintage creations. "Our desire is to create machines that have so much character, they feel alive, needing to be tamed—anthropomorphic instruments you must develop visceral relationships with in order not to kill you," explains Borras. El Solitario also sells a carefully curated selection of gear that complements the spirit of their bikes, such as leather accessories, clothing in rugged wools and cotton, and handcrafted silver jewelry.

ON THE ROAD CHECKLIST

1

2

1. PENDLETON: There is nothing like a Pendleton blanket to keep out the chill when sitting around the campfire after a long day's ride. For over a century, Pendleton Woolen Mills in Oregon has been known for its quality wool blankets, apparel, and accessories, with patterns drawn from Native American culture and Scottish tartans. ___2. 3SIXTEEN X HCR: For the perfect cuppa wherever you go, New York designers 3Sixteen partnered with Los Angeles Handsome Coffee Roasters to create the limited edition 3Sixteen x HCR Travel Coffee Kit. Each bag is handmade in Vashon, Washington by Teppei Teranishi using brass hardware and elegant, water-resistant Chromexcel leather from the world famous Horween Tannery in Chicago. The kits ship with an Aeropress and filters, a bag of freshly roasted Handsome Roasters coffee beans, a Porlex mini hand grinder, and an AWS digital scale.

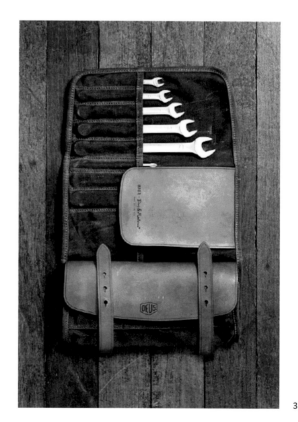

1. BMD DESIGN: Bruno Michaud of BMD Design in Bordeaux France channels his passion for café racing culture and retro hand lettering onto these custom designed vintage motorcycle helmets. ___ 2. FARMERS RACER: Clean-lined and functional, the handcrafted packbags by Farmer's Racer in Sweden recall days of yore. Handcrafting his limited edition packbags and backpacks from waxed cotton canvas using hand tools and vintage Singer sewing machines, Swedish designer Lars Gustavsson is building his brand on the icon of the Swedish racing farmer. ___ 3. MAKR X DEUS: 15 tool pockets and 2 utility pouches in the Makr x Deus Tool Roll lovingly hold all you need to strip down an engine by the side of the road. Developed by motorcycle brand Deus ex Machina in collaboration with Makr Carry Goods from Florida, each roll is handcrafted from waxed canvas and American harness leather.

1

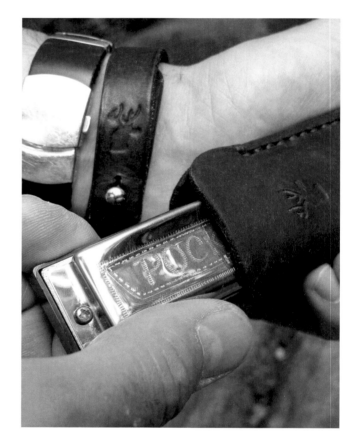

3

2

1. FIELD NOTES: Using pen and paper to record one's thoughts offers a haptic immediacy that cannot be replaced by modern electronics. Field Notes pocket notebooks pay tribute to such joys of the analog era in both function and form. ___ 2. BOKER: An all-in-one cutlery solution for eating on the go, the Magnum Bon Appetite by Boker features individually locking knife, fork, and spoon in 440 stainless steel and a black wood handle for a classic look. ___ 3. BUSH SMARTS: Contribute to the songs of the wilderness with the Bush Smarts Camp Harmonica. The oiled leather sheath handmade in New York carries a folk/country style harmonica in the key of C by Hohner of Germany.

1. LEATHERMAN: For a quarter of a century, Oregon-based Leatherman has been producing multifunctional pocket tools for the practically minded. The story of the Oregon-based company began when founder Tim Leatherman realized that a pair of pliers on his pocket knife would be a great addition. The Surge is one of Leatherman's two largest multi-tools, featuring 21 tough tools and the company's customary 25-year warranty. ___ 2. EL SOLITARIO: El Solitario's Limited Edition Silk Scarf celebrates the fierce independence of bikers and adventurers, as seen in Dutch artist Menze Kwint. Produced in France, in collaboration with Lyon silk scarf makers A Piece Of Chic. ___ 3. BUSH SMARTS: The Game Kit by New York outdoor brand Bush Smarts contains everything you need to play cards, roll dice, or scratch your own game on the waterproof score pad in the customizable tin. ___ 4. BUSH SMARTS: Taking up practically no space in your pack, the Flat Pack Bowl by Bush Smarts needs just three folds to become a watertight bowl. Holes make it easy to hold hot foods and hang it up to dry.

S N O W

"Look deep into nature,
and then you will understand
everything better."

Albert Einstein

David Boyson Cooper

Anki Grothe

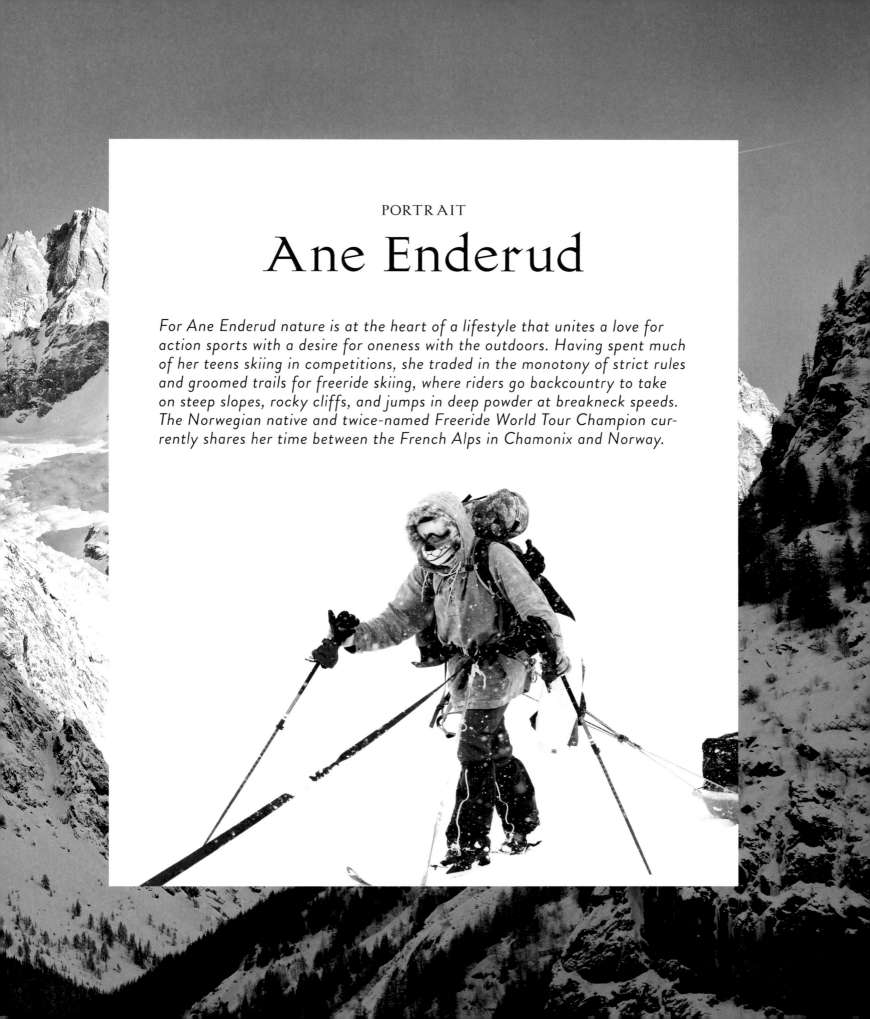

PORTRAIT

Ane Enderud

For Ane Enderud nature is at the heart of a lifestyle that unites a love for action sports with a desire for oneness with the outdoors. Having spent much of her teens skiing in competitions, she traded in the monotony of strict rules and groomed trails for freeride skiing, where riders go backcountry to take on steep slopes, rocky cliffs, and jumps in deep powder at breakneck speeds. The Norwegian native and twice-named Freeride World Tour Champion currently shares her time between the French Alps in Chamonix and Norway.

What motivated you to pursue freeride skiing over on-piste skiing or snowboarding?

The sense of freedom without so many rules and systems affecting the experience, and personal growth.

Please describe your most extreme freeride experience.

My most extreme freeride experience was a variation on a line I did in Chamonix a few years ago. I made the most technical turns I had ever done in my life, and there was absolutely no room for even the slightest mistake. But what frightened me the most was my crash in the summer of 2009, which injured me severely. I had a lot of speed when I hit an ice chunk at the bottom of my run, which sent me off like a cannon. I landed on the ice with my neck, shoulders, and upper back first. Today I am very thankful that the damage on my spine from the impact incredibly has been possible to reverse and heal.

Growing up in Norway the outdoors figured large in your childhood. Do you remember what you loved most about the outdoors when you were a kid? What you loved doing most?

I was outside as much as possible and was always attracted to a variety of activities as a child. I really loved climbing trees, ice skating, and sledding. In the summers I loved to water ski, play ball games, and practice archery. I have been told it was always hard to get me in for dinner! I grew up in Oslo near the mountains, and my parents introduced me to skiing on the weekends and holidays in nearby Hemsedal. When I started alpine skiing, the tree skiing and trails with natural jumps and obstacles was my favorite.

Now that you are an adult, what does being in the outdoors mean for you?

Energy and freedom. Being in harmony with nature at a more conscious level. I still love action, but I don't need more than the quiet of nature to feel balanced. Being outdoors is at the heart of my lifestyle and that will never change.

Anki Grøthe is working on a photo series called "Nature Ladies" that you have been a part of. Can you tell us a bit about that project and what makes it so special?

The idea has been to spend more time in the nature with my girlfriends. We decided to learn how to be independent in the outback and inspire other girls to believe in their own capacity to be safe in nature. I believe that all of us as human beings, and especially us girls when it comes to sports and practical lifestyles, are greatly limited by our own fear. It's a very destructive emotion for learning and growth. I also want to show that, despite my world champion title, I need to work all the time to stay in a fearless and open state of mind so I can learn for myself where my limits are. You need to push your boundaries to know what you are capable of. We live in a time filled with fear, and it keeps us from not living to our greatest potential.

Successful athletes are always role models as well. As a young, female, champion freeride skier, you can't help but inspire more women and girls to enter the seemingly male dominated world of outdoors and action sports. How do you see that and what would you say is your impact?

My impression is that the gender balance in snow sports at least, and especially freeride skiing and snowboarding, has changed radically over the last 10 years. There are so many more girls out there playing and searching for action and experiences in nature. It is still not balanced in the movies and media when compared to the actual amount of girls ripping out in the mountains these days. In Norway I see a huge interest among girls to learn more so they also can feel confident in the mountains. For the last two years I have also been working as a coach and have noticed a lot of interest for ladies-only courses, where they can learn in their own way and at their own speed. And I could immediately sense a difference in the focus: on having a good total experience with nice breaks with food and talk, instead of a rushed feeling of competition all the time. I think this is a good development for everyone—we could use more female energy in action sports!

Your passion and skill in freeride skiing has taken you to some magnificent locations. What is the most amazing place you've been to for skiing and what made it so special for you?

That's a difficult question! Many places and experiences have a special place in my heart. But Svalbard, Norway stands out as a very unique trip. It is the most remote place I have skied in, and the feeling of wilderness and freedom was amazing. For 10 days we were based on a sailboat, and we travelled through the archipelago searching for unskied terrain. The arctic landscape with its ancient wilderness was incredible to experience. It's a trip I will never forget.

When you are out for a day trip in the backcountry, what gear do you always take with you?

My backpack always has safety gear. A first-aid kit, water, some extra snacks, and a wool blanket in case I end up being outside longer than planned. I also carry a probe, shovel, and an emergency beacon.

What's on your to-do list for the upcoming year?

I have so many dreams to fulfill, and I am excited to see which one of them will come true next! But the underlying

"We could use
more female energy in
action sports!"

Photographs on this and the following pages by Anki Grøthe

focus is being happy and healthy. To continue being curious about what life has to offer, to stay alert and learn with an open mind. I just started studying Qigong and I got my scuba diving license last fall, so those are two new activities I will devote some time to in the next years. I've also been reading all I can about leading a balanced, healthy, and happy life. I believe in working towards a more free and clean planet and have some projects linked to this subject that I hope will be started in the upcoming months.

Steep slopes, rough cold terrain, the threat of injury and avalanches—how about outdoor activities that are less extreme?

I usually do a lot of action sports all year round, like downhill biking, surfing, and climbing. But in the last couple of years I have travelled less, and have rediscovered how much I love simply being outdoors in nature. It is so peaceful and energizing. It's where I really connect with myself.

Anki Grøthe

"Taking images is a result of my cravings," commented Norwegian photographer Anki Grøthe. Following her studies in photography she moved to Hemsedal, surrounding herself with the natural beauty of the small mountain village known for its skiing, snowboarding, and fly-fishing. Her portraits and documentary photographs capture the raw wilderness of nature and the human emotion that abounds in its presence.

Niche

Snowboarders use the mountains so why not try to give a little back? Since launching in 2010, Niche has created light, snappy, eco-friendly boards in eye-catching designs and color-ways that have quickly won a strong fanbase as well as international awards. Niche points out that their unique material combinations and production techniques not only reduce their impact on the environment, they also increase performance. Non-toxic bio-resin adds liveliness and strength, while recyclable basalt fibers replace fiberglass to make the boards stronger and lighter than conventional ones.

Kilian Schönberger

It might be said that Kilian Schönberger's childhood exploring the woods behind his home had a formative influence on his work today. His alpine landscapes and fairytale forests convey a melancholic and raw beauty that awakens a sense of longing for places and times far removed from daily life in the concrete jungle. An almost painterly romanticism is balanced by his keen sense of composition, lighting, and structure—an awareness, he points out, that might be heightened by his colorblindness. Based in Cologne, Germany, he studied geography in Bonn and works as a landscape and architecture photographer and writer.

Arved Fuchs

*The first man to reach both the North Pole and the South Pole by foot in
a single year, German explorer Arved Fuchs earned the nickname "Ice Fox" through
his many Arctic expeditions by sailboat, kayak, skis, and dogsled. He has
written numerous books, lectured about his extreme and spectacular journeys, and
is outspoken on issues surrounding climate change and global warming.*

People spend time in the outdoors for all sorts of reasons—for the thrill, to be close to nature, to save the world. What is it that drives you all the way to the ends of the earth?

I always loved being in the great outdoors. Cut free from the shackles of modern technology, just nature, pure. Of course there is the thrill of adventure, and the physical challenges. But I have also always been curious. To be in nature and experience all that it has to offer.

How did your upbringing affect your relationship to the outdoors today?

I grew up in a small village in Schleswig Holstein (the northernmost state in Germany). I was constantly outdoors. We didn't have a television when I was a child but a house full of books. And many of them were about adventurers and explorers like James Cook and Roald Amundsen. Reading about them as a boy was inspiring, and I swore to myself that one day, I would be just like them. I always kept my goal ahead of me and never let the doubts of others get in the way. Doing what I do now is a dream come true.

Extreme travel into snow and ice—what equipment is necessary to meet the particular challenges in such an environment?

I wouldn't focus on the equipment per se. Every trip is different. Of course a sleeping bag and protective clothes. But what is needed really depends on what you are prepared to do, and what you can do. A lot of people think that they'll be prepared if they have the most, and the most expensive gear, but it's not true. You have to ask yourself: "What can I do, where are my bounds?" I've seen beginners completely overdressed for the Arctic, and then they find themselves sweating and then freezing as a result. Thorough research and intensive preparation for one's trip and destination are essential.

What pieces of outdoor gear do you never leave your house without?

I don't need a survival kit when I'm at home! I look at these things pragmatically: it depends on the task at hand. If I'm out on the weekend for a quick sail or kayaking, I'll probably have a small pocketknife with me, a lighter, and some matches. But not if I'm going to the opera with my wife. Or to the airport, for that matter—they won't let me carry those on to the airplane!

What does the work-life balance look like for a professional adventurer?

I don't separate work and fun in the traditional sense—I have the great luck to be able to make a living from my hobby. An expedition is not simply done when I return from a trip. There is a lot of following up to do—evaluating the trip, then preparing lectures—and then for the next trips there is a lot of planning to do, from bureaucracy and financing to organizing the right equipment, to getting in shape for the trip and getting the team together. In general I try to do one or two expeditions per year. It depends on how long each one is.

"I don't need a survival kit when I'm at home!"

You mention a team; can you elaborate on that a bit?

I travelled solo when I was just starting out, but I found it a bit monotonous. I find teamwork important. I really enjoy working together with different people and their individual characters, leading them into challenging situations. There are usually about ten of us on a trip, sometimes as few as four if I'm on my sailboat the Dagmar.

That is probably so much more important when your travels take you to such remote areas …

Yes, but we do encounter people—I have had a lot of contact with the Inuit on my trips. They are few and live in small settlements. It's not the quantity but the quality of the encounter that counts. I am sure there are millions of fascinating people in New York City, but what interests me are indigenous populations who live so close to nature.

At what point did you decide to address climate change in your work? How can you make a difference?

I have been doing expeditions for nearly 30 years. And in that time I have naturally witnessed the impact that our actions have had on nature. In addition to having outdoor adventures and challenges, my love for nature has always been part of the equation. I don't just want to bring back beautiful photographs, but see it as my duty to serve as an advocate for this nature that has given me—all of us—so much. But concretely—in the early nineties I started undertaking Arctic expeditions by sailboat on the Dagmar Aaen, trying to sail the Northwest and Northeast passages. Throughout history, these passages have been known as notoriously hazardous to cross. We often had to turn back because of the ice. Even at the end of the nineties I would not have believed in global warming. But just a few years later, I could hardly believe my eyes. By 2002, there was hardly any ice left in the Northwest Passage. Today scores of boats, even cruise ships pass through it without a problem. At first you think it's just a stroke of luck or due to the irregularity of nature. But then when you compare your own experience with scientific reports, you realize that there's a serious problem.

What expedition are you most proud of and why?

Well, I am proud of the fact that I am the first person to have reached both Poles by foot. It's an impressive feat physically, but actually in the larger scheme of things it's not that important …

Could you describe the most beautiful moment you've experienced in the outdoors?

I don't look for that—I don't have a vacation complex where I want to collect experiences that are "the most" this or that. Every project has moments where you experience fear or danger, but then also times of being in complete harmony with oneself and with nature. When you don't have to do a thing but be. Call it a spiritual moment. I've found beauty everywhere. Take Greenland, which also has a wonderful cultural history and delightful people. And then Antarctica, and the South Seas—the whole world is so majestic, which is why we have to preserve it. The saying that that we need nature and not the other way around is more true than ever.

> "I don't have a vacation complex where I want to collect experiences that are 'the most' this or that."

What outdoor adventure is still on your to do list?

I'm going to keep on having adventures for as long as I can! I can't talk about specifics at the moment since we are still in the research process, but I can say that we are working on a longer trip to Antarctica for 2015.

Coming back to the environment. What can you do to make a difference?

I've always been a very political person. And so I voice my opinions where I can. But I also asked myself that question. In addition to talking, how could I become active to effect change in society? So eight years ago, I came up with the Ice Climate Education (I.C.E.) Program. Our mission is to make young people around the world aware of global warming and its effects through hands-on experience in the Arctic regions. Young people aged 16 to 19 can apply through a competition and about ten are then selected for the ten-day program. Starting last year, we have held part of the camp on board a sailing ship. Volunteer scientists teach them about climate change and marine conservation, and they do excursions on land as well. We've held the camp in Norway and Iceland, and 2014 will be our eighth consecutive year doing the camp. All costs are covered—Jack Wolfskin is a major sponsor—and the staff (myself included) donates their time.

Nordisk

A hiker's three heaviest items are usually the backpack, the sleeping system (bag and mat), and the shelter. While minimalists may embrace the prospects of sleeping in a hammock or under a tarp, others may not want to abstain from the enclosure of a tent. For the latter, Danish outdoor company Nordisk created its Telemark series of ultra-lightweight tents. A recent recipient of the Red Dot Design Award, the Telemark combines state-of-the-art technology and decades of dealing with Scandinavia's harsh outdoor climate to achieve a superb combination of design, form, and function. Boasting a weight of only 880 g, the single pole tent unfolds from a pack size of only 12 × 35 cm to an interior of 220 × 135 × 100 cm. With practice it can be pitched in less than four minutes. Having been a name in the European outdoor industry for a long time, Nordisk's comprehensive product range includes tents, sleeping bags, backpacks, and other outdoor gear.

Tal Roberts

Based in the ski mecca of Ketchum, Idaho, Tal Roberts channels his passion for the outdoor lifestyle through his lens. His images capture the exhilarating spirit and talent of skiers, skateboarders, and BMXers against the stunning backdrops that are their stage, from the concrete curves of a half-pipe at dusk, to a brilliant landscape of snow-covered mountain peaks spreading into infinity. His work can be seen in gallery exhibits as well as campaigns for outdoor brands such as Smith and Scott Sports.

Vincent Stanley

Having worked for Patagonia for some 40 years since its inception in 1973, Vincent Stanley pretty much knows the company inside and out. The marketing vice president works "on the intersection of product and environmental stories." He helped initiate and lead the company's Footprint Chronicles, Common Threads Initiative, and, together with Patagonia founder Yvon Chouinard, co-wrote the visionary book **The Responsible Company: What We've Learned from Patagonia's First 40 Years.**

Patagonia is a brand created by and for people who love the outdoors. What is your personal way of spending time outdoors? What does being outdoors mean to you?

When I came to work for my uncle Yvon Chouinard at his climbing shop 40 years ago, I was the only nonclimber, nonsurfer among a small band of machinists, blacksmiths, and hammer makers. Over time, of course, I tried, at least once, every activity we made gear or clothes for, but I never fell in love with any particular sport. I

did fall in love with the mountains and the sea. Now my wife and I cross-country ski every winter in the North Cascades and hike there every summer. Every summer we sea kayak in Merchants Row along the coast of Maine. It means the world to me to get some distance from the road or just a bit away from the sand, to feel vulnerable to the weather, rockslides, or lightning.

Patagonia takes a very particular stance when it comes to saving the environment. Can you tell us when and how this started and how you see it developing in the future?

As climbers and surfers, Yvon and his tribe could sense before most people the environmental degradation that attended the explosion of population and economic activity in the sixties and beyond. They could see the glaciers melting when they returned to climb Kilimanjaro, or see 1,000-year-old sequoias wilting from L.A. smog. When you love wilderness, you want to protect it. By the 1980s the Chouinards had begun donating 1% of sales, in good years and bad, to grassroots environmental organizations working to save a particular patch of land or stretch of river. It took us longer to understand how much we rely, back home in the city, on the vitality of local ecosystems and fight to protect, for instance, the health of the river that runs right by our headquarters. It took us even longer to push back the curtain between us and our supply chain, to look at the social and environmental implications of everything done in our name to produce our clothes. We started with the switch from conventional to organic cotton and virgin to recycled polyester, then introduced our Common Threads partnership and our end-of-product-life take-back program. Now we are working with other businesses through the Sustainable Apparel Coalition to take baseline measurements of energy and water use and greenhouse gases and waste generated, then apply continuous improvements to reduce harm and improve resource efficiency. The hope eventually is for a consumer-facing social and environmental scorecard for each product.

How has Patagonia managed to stick to its mission despite its widespread success as a company?

Patagonia has never been sold, for one thing. The Chouinards, with the rest of the company 20 years ago, adopted a mission statement that calls on us all to "build the best product, cause no unnecessary harm, and use business to implement and inspire solutions to the environmental crisis." This represented who we were, both owners and employees, in 1992. And those words represent us even more now: they are woven so deeply into the culture and history of the company. We have learned more how to live by them. In 2012, we became a B Corp, which enabled us to write our values into the charter and by-laws of our company permanently, even if the company were to be sold by the family.

Mikey Schaefer

What advice would you give to startups in the outdoor retail industry who are looking to balance vision with profit?

The outdoor business is crowded. Make or sell something excellent that people need and can't get elsewhere. Product performance and quality have to come first. But in our time, quality includes care for nature and for the community as well as your employees and customers. Don't wait till you make your first profit to realize that. You'll gain much needed practice and knowledge (some of it money-saving) by being conscious businesspeople from the start.

The trend to value quality over disposable, handmade over mass-produced, even the revival in heritage styles of clothes and bags—where do you see this as coming from? Is it just a fad—like the retro trend apparent in so many areas of culture, or does this signal a true shift in mentality?

We have both things at work: retro style is a fad, or looks like one from my vantage point of having seen the "outdoor look" come and go over the decades. But the embracing of

quality by millennials and rejection of consumption as addictive entertainment—I think, I hope, that's with us to stay.

What was your most beautiful and extreme moment in nature?

I remember lying in my sleeping bag in the sand by the Salmon River in Idaho on a cold summer night, third day into a raft trip, staring at the stars, nowhere sleepy. I was in my late 20s and had never been so far from a road. What I saw was so beautiful, so powerfully present, I felt unequal to it. I thought my heart would break. I thought, this world is so perfect, I can't stand it; then I could.

What outdoor adventure is still on your to do list?

A hut-to-hut week in the Alps. Not much of an adventure, but what I'd like to do.

What pieces of outdoor gear do you never leave your house without?

I should name a favorite Patagonia thing. I have several, but nothing I never leave behind.

"Build the best product, cause no unnecessary harm, and use business to implement and inspire solutions to the environmental crisis."

Celebrating its 40th anniversary in 2013, Patagonia has issued the Legacy Collection, a capsule collection of 10 iconic creations from Patagonia's early years, reinterpreted with modern materials and a more refined fit while maintaining the original aesthetic. Here, a few of the original vintage pieces (left) alongside their Special Edition counterparts (right): Summit Pack; All-Wear Down Jacket; Post Foamback Cagoule.

SNOW CHECKLIST

1. YETI: For snowy adventures in the mountains or about town, German-Danish brand Yeti offers some of the lightest most breathable, packable, weatherproof, and ethically sourced down products available. ___ 2. ROAM & SEEK: The Official R&S Vintage Trawler Style Beanie in 100 % acrylic warms your head with a good conscience. London-based Roam & Seek makes ethically produced apparel inspired by snowboarding, skateboarding, and surfing.

1. MTN APPROACH: For snowboarders wanting to access backcountry powder without the uphill trudge in snowshoes or having to swap their favorite board for a heavy splitboard, MTN Approach of Ketchum, Idaho have come up with a solution. The MTN Approach System features two lightweight, foldable skis with pre-attached skins and universal bindings along with a custom backpack to carry the gear plus your snowboard. Also available as a full Winter Kit, which includes the above system plus touring poles, a probe, and shovel. ___
2. SALEWA: Italian brand Salewa pours over 75 years of alpine gear production into its Rapace GTX Trekking Boot. With a lightweight design for light mountaineering and hiking: the sole provides enough stiffness for use with crampons but also agility and traction to negotiate rough terrain and slippery surfaces. ___ 3. POLER X MIZU: Oregon-based outdoor brand Poler is one of several high profile action sports brands to partner with Mizu to champion the stainless steel water bottle as an alternative to disposable plastic bottles. 1% of the proceeds from the Poler x Mizu water bottle line is donated to the nonprofit water.org.

1. YETI: Keeping you cozy when every bit of space counts, the Yeti VIB 1000 down sleeping bag is the warmest in the Yeti Very Important Bag range of ultralight sleeping bags, made from best European goose down filling and SupCell, an incredibly thin and robust nylon material.___2. CANADA GOOSE: For a warm head in cold weather extremes, the iconic aviator hat by Canada Goose brings together the best of old and new. With a traditional coyote fur ruff visor and earflaps, a buckle chinstrap, and Arctic-tech fabric for durability and weather resistance.___3. SPOT: A personal locator beacon (PLB) can be a matter of life or death when you're stuck in the outback. Operating on the GEOS private satellite network, the SPOT Gen3 Satellite GPS Messenger tracks your location and lets you send messages or an emergency responder to your GPS location at the push of a button. While the service comes with a price—the cost of the device plus annual subscription for the customized tracking services—it could well be worth the peace of mind.___4. NORDISK: The newest tent by Nordisk released in 2014, the Faxe Trekking Tent offers a 3-in-1 construction in a classic tent design: use the inner tent made of robust Technical Cotton (a cotton/polyester blend) or the outer nylon tent shelter separately, or combined according to weather and preference. Available in two sizes for two or four persons.

1

2

3

1. NATIONAL FOREST: Ladies only. Los Angeles design studio National Forest teamed up with women-specific snowboard brand Roxy Snow to bring color and cheer to its recent snowboard collection.___2. NORSE PROJECTS: Warm up in style with the Ivar Scarf by Danish brand Norse Projects. The fair isle-inspired pattern is woven from 100% Scottish Knoll merino yarn. ___3. ETÓN CORP.: In an emergency, the Boost Turbine 4000 by California-based Etón Corporation can be a lifesaver. Hand cranking the internal 4,000 mAh lithium ion battery for a minute will generate enough power to make a 30-second phone call or send and receive a few text messages. Lightweight and compact, it can also be charged at home and taken along as an extra battery pack. Winner of the Good Design Award 2013, it includes a mini and regular USB port and a light indicator for battery charge level.

WATER

"Live in each season as it passes; breathe the air, drink the drink, taste the fruit, and resign yourself to the influence of the earth."

Henry David Thoreau

Wood & Faulk

Ever been out and about and in need of a quick bite or a spontaneous sit down? Wood & Faulk might have the solution. Inspired by the old and the new, the classics and the future classics, the Portland-based company brings together functionality and aesthetics through the unique vision of its maker. Owner Matt Pierce launched Wood & Faulk in 2010 as a blog for documenting his projects, ideas, and do-it-yourself creations. It has since evolved into a small company where Matt and his supporting team of three handcraft and sell limited-run products derived from the blog and items used in the workshop. The iconic Camp Stool, derived from one of Pierce's first and most popular DIY projects, the inventive Heritage Charcuterie Sheath for carrying a knife and sausage, and the do-it-yourself cheeseboard are just a few of the highlights.

Norquay

A small island nestled in the North Channel of Canada's Lake Huron, Norquay is also the name Natasha Wittke chose to name her new company for the formative role it has in her life as the site of her first solo camping experience. Bringing together an enthusiasm for the great outdoors with her affinity for design, Natasha Wittke launched Norquay in Montreal as a brand dedicated to the art of camping, applying new design ideas to traditional items.

Reflecting Wittke's passion for canoeing, Norquay launched in 2013 with a series of handcrafted, handpainted canoe paddles whose colors and patterns are inspired by the beauty and heritage of Northern Canada. The cherry wood paddles are produced by Teal Paddles in New Liskeard, Ontario, and then sent for handpainting and staining by a small team of artisans at the Norquay studio in Montreal.

Áetem

Traditionally, exploring the natural treasures that edge the earth's coastlines can involve hiking along cliffs, travelling their length in a boat, and swimming or snorkeling in select locations—before returning to the point of departure to switch gear or set up camp. Now, there is a movement to both simplify coastal exploration and expand its scope: seatrekking.

This new outdoor sport involves hiking and camping in coastal areas and then swimming, snorkeling, or free diving across stretches of water to follow a route otherwise unavailable to travelers on foot or boat alone. Founded by passionate seatrekker Bernhard Wache in 2011, German company Áetem has created on/off-shore waterproof packs aimed at travellers looking to explore the seacoasts and take their gear with them, no matter where they go.

The idea of seatrekking is based on a principle of reduction in order to travel independently, spontaneously, and in accordance with nature. Only the most necessary gear is stowed in the packs and carried on the back while on land or attached to the ankle with a leash, floating along as you explore the seafloor. Equipment and provisions are selected so as not to leave a trace behind. Nights are spent ashore beneath the stars.

For over 15 years, Áetem's founder has been an avid snorkeler and freediver. Driven by the desire to go on tours that lasted more than a day, Wache confronted the issue of how to take his luggage with him. Finding nothing adequate on the market, he set about designing a pack that would fit his needs to a t. Six years later, his 70-liter James C. was awarded the Brandnew Award at the 2013 ISPO (International Trade Fair For Sports Equipment and Fashion) in Munich and went into production later that year.

In addition to the big pack designed for multi-day tours is the 35-liter Falcon S. daypack. Both are made from a waterproof, tear-resistant outer material with two adjustable chambers for wet and dry gear. A patented valve system allows you to inflate the pack when you are ready to swim, and adjust the stiffness of the pack for carrying comfort on the back. The bags include an adaptive anchoring system which keep them in place if you choose to freedive and explore the water's depths. An attachable diving flag alerts others to your whereabouts.

Áetem's flagship Sea Shell Charles D. is a high-performance multitasker in carbon fiber. Removable aluminum fins provide agility and control to the 65-liter aquadynamic hardshell, which also serves well as a bodyboard. Optional wheels turn the made-to-order backpack into a trolley.

For those in search of inspiration for their next (or first) seatrekking adventure, Áetem provides a list of favorite routes on its website, including trip reports, maps, gear lists, and photos.

Mark Kalch

*Australian-born Mark Kalch is a professional expedition kayaker and a storyteller using words and images. He has explored jungles in East Africa, walked alone across Iran, and rafted the entire Amazon River from the Peruvian Andes to the Atlantic Ocean. With his **7 Rivers, 7 Continents** project he aims to paddle the length of the longest river on each continent. When he is not exploring the wilderness he can be found most recently with his family in Buenos Aires, keeping in condition with Jiu-Jitsu, and developing a line of technical clothing designed for expedition paddlers.*

How did your upbringing influence your love for the outdoors?

I was fortunate to grow up on the shores of the Pacific Ocean in Queensland, Australia. In our front yard we had the endless emerald sea and in our backyard the quintessential Aussie bush stretched forever. In a small town we were forced as much by love as by necessity to find some way to amuse ourselves outdoors. Being outside, barefoot, and in a pair of board shorts was just a pretty natural way to be. I never wanted to change that.

How did you get into paddling? Was there a moment or experience that made you say, "this is it" over other sports?

Paddling didn't take hold until I spent my first season whitewater river guiding in South Africa. For weeks at a time we paddled and worked hard under the desert sun. At night we camped beside the river under a billion stars. The simplicity of life drew me in. When you are on river not much else matters. I liked that. I still like that.

You share your experiences through writing, speaking, and audiovisually. What is the beauty or purpose of human-powered adventures that you want to convey to others?

Oneness. Travelling by human power alone affords an interaction with your surroundings like no other and offers endless opportunities for exploration. You are literally "in touch" with the planet and people. Paddling a river, you become part of it. Invited for a meal in a stranger's home on a long journey, you become a part of, however briefly, their lives. This time spent up close and personal with the outdoors lends an understanding to life on earth that I don't think can be achieved otherwise.

You have taken on the formidable task of paddling "source to sea" on the longest river of each continent. What river is up next, when, and how long do you think it will take compared to the Amazon and the Missouri-Mississippi?

In June 2014, as part of my *7 Rivers 7 Continents* project, I will make a paddling descent of the Volga River in Russia. At nearly 3,700 km, it is Europe's longest and largest river. Pinning down exactly how long it will take is difficult. You can estimate based on the type of river, speed of flow, its length, of course, but there are so many variables as to make it only a rough guess. The Amazon River descent took 153 days and the Missouri-Mississippi River 117 days. Both these rivers are over 6,000 km long. Surely the Volga will take no time at all? Not exactly. I don't put much emphasis on getting from A to B or source to sea quickly as possible. They really just give me a start and end point. What happens in between is much more important. There are photos to take, people to meet, and experiences to live. It's a balancing act for sure.

How does family figure into the life of an outdoor expeditionist? Do the outdoors figure into everyday life? What about family outdoor adventures?

Having a young family while away for five or six months at a time on expedition is tough. No matter how difficult things get on a big journey, by far the hardest part is being away from them. We currently live in Buenos Aires, Argentina, which really puts the pressure on to get outdoors as much as we would like when I am home. Our biggest saving grace is being able to visit the Paraná Delta, a huge network of islands and wetlands close to the city. The kids have a great time where we can camp, kayak, and visit friends. Keeping the children in close contact with the outdoors is hugely important to us.

What is the most essential outdoor advice you would give your kids?

My advice to the kids, all kids, would be to connect with the outdoors. Swim, run, jump, climb, paddle, surf, camp, and explore the world. It is outside where you will find answers to most things in life.

Your expeditions take you to a range of climates and conditions, so of course you pack accordingly. But do you have a core survival kit of gear or accessories you take with you no matter where? What does it consist of?

Of course it depends upon conditions but I do keep a few items on me at all times as a kind of survival kit. I wear mostly board shorts, a long sleeve UV shirt, water shoes, cap, and sunglasses. It's my uniform on a big paddle. I also use a Suunto Ambit2 wristop computer, which gives me data on everything from elevation and exact location to weather

conditions and heart rate. To this outfit I add a small 20-liter Seal Line dry bag. It's a durable, PVC-free, 300D polyester bag, double urethane coated with roll top and buckle. In here you keep anything you don't want to get wet. It's stored in the kayak cockpit and is the first thing to reach for in an emergency.

It generally contains: *Lowe Alpine lightweight rain gear, Lowe Alpine thermal underwear, Petzl headlamp, Benchmade folding knife, Olympus Tough camera, lighter, chocolate bars, Ibuprofen, passport/documents, phone, money/cards, head scarf, throw bag, and carabiners.*

With these items I can endure and hopefully extract myself from most difficult and unexpected situations.

Please describe your ideal outdoor meal and setting.

My ideal outdoor meal and setting could be one spent alone, far from anywhere, or with old friends and new. Some

"Having a young family while away for five or six months at a time on expedition is tough. No matter how difficult things get on a big journey, by far the hardest part is being away from them."

of the most memorable outdoor meals I have had were while I sat on rocky ledges in the Zagros Mountains of Iran, eating stale bread and canned stew with not a soul for miles. Or beside a fast flowing river, boats pulled to the side, bbq in full swing, and friends swapping tall tales of exploit.

What was your most frightening, dangerous, or extreme outdoor experience? Would you do it again?

On the upper Amazon River in Peru, we descended the river, Apurimac, which, translated from Quechuan, can mean the "Divine Voice" or "Voice of God." It is a difficult whitewater river, upon which we endured days and weeks of capsize, near misses, and narrow escapes. All of our small team (just three of us) quite literally saved each other's lives on a number of occasions. I would do it again and will have to endure the same and more on the upper reaches of the Nile and Yangtze Rivers. A prospect which both excites and terrifies me.

Having seen so much of it, what is your favorite place on earth and why?

Choosing just one place is a difficult assignment indeed! In 2010, I walked across the Islamic Republic of Iran from the Caspian Sea in the north to the Persian Gulf in the south, a distance of around 1,700 km. On my journey I passed through dense green jungle, small villages, and giant cities. I crossed dry desert plateau and enormous snow covered mountain ranges. Along the way I met the people of Iran. I stayed in their homes, ate with them, spoke with them, and laughed with them. I was fortunate to discover and document a country very different to the one presented via negative media and political propaganda. Never had I encountered a country with a more diverse and beautiful geography. Endless mountains to climb, deserts to cross, and even rivers to paddle. But it has become my favorite place on earth because of its people. Their genuine hospitality, friendship, and caring knows no bounds.

17·3·13

Ben Lamb

The abundance of wildlife and vintage outdoor adventure magazines, not to mention popular culture in all its expressions, regularly inspire the work of Manchester-based illustrator and designer Ben Lamb. Highly detailed drawings done by hand and collage are the central techniques of his work and process.

Andy Grellmann

The quiet, pensive atmosphere conveyed in the landscapes and personal moments that Andy Grellmann captures with his lens on analog film inspire to find one's own private paradise in nature. Born and raised in Vancouver, Canada, Grellmann has found many of his motifs close to home along the west coast and interior of British Columbia.

Oru Kayak

Architect and product designer Anton Willis grew up paddling in the lakes and rivers of Mendocino County, California. In 2008, a move to a small apartment in San Francisco forced him to put his fiberglass kayak in storage. A magazine article about origami, the Japanese art of paper folding, inspired him to apply the same principle to make a real boat that he could keep at home. Five years on, the Oru Kayak is in full production in California and shipped worldwide. Made from corrugated polypropylene and ABS plastic, it features an origami skin with folding creases permanently molded in. The lightweight kayak folds into its own carrying case with space to hold a life vest, the four-piece Oru Paddle, and more. Fully recyclable, it uses 70% less petroleum to manufacture than a standard kayak.

Experiment with Nature

As the tagline of Shwood wooden eyewear company in Portland, Oregon, "Experiment with Nature" describes the ethos of the people behind the brand. It is also the name of the Shwood blog, where they share their many creative side projects and inspirations with the wider community. As its name suggests, many of these efforts have an outdoor bend. Pictured here is the renovation of an old canoe using simple hardware store supplies. Shwood founder Eric Singer transformed it into a top-notch water vessel, perfect for paddling in Trillium Lake against the backdrop of Mount Hood.

Sanborn Canoe

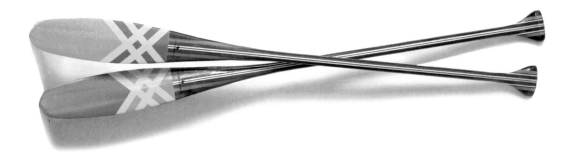

While paddles have a primarily functional purpose, their quality and aesthetics can transform a paddling experience into an expression of a life well lived. Those who appreciate the liveliness, warmth, and natural beauty of handcarved wood over plastic, aluminum, or carbon fiber paddles will certainly appreciate the artisanry of Sanborn Canoe Company. The small company in Winona, Minnesota was founded in 2009 by a group of devoted canoeists. Each of their wooden paddles for canoes and kayaks is handcrafted using laminated combinations of the finest woods, like red and white cedar, ash, and cherry, selected both for aesthetics and durability. Uniting the heritage of paddle making with modern-day advancements, the blades are wrapped in fiberglass and coated in epoxy for added strength and durability.

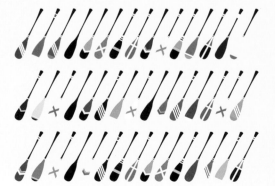

SANBORN CANOE COMPANY

HANDCRAFTED IN WINONA. MINNESOTA

McLellan Jacobs

Carbon fiber is prized as a material for high-performance vehicles in the aerospace, automotive, and boat making industries. As its technology advances and prices lower, it is increasingly being seen in the likes of bicycles, canoes, and kayaks. New Zealand designer Jamie McLellan, who also worked with Avanti on their high performance carbon fiber bicycles, teamed up with designer Andy Jacobs to create the Kayak 1. The single person, recreational kayak is not only lightweight—weighing in at around 16 kg—but also top of the line when it comes to luxury. Constructed by America's Cup yacht builders in New Zealand, Kayak 1 sports a gloss carbon finish, gold-plated brass fittings, and teak timberwork. For a truly bespoke product, different colors, materials, and finishes can also be ordered to spec.

BioLite

To avoid being completely cut off from civilization while in the woods or even at home during a power outage, the BioLite CampStove offers an environmentally conscious solution. The compact biomass stove burns wood chips, twigs, pinecones, and the like and in the process generates electricity. This powers a fan to efficiently create a small but hot, low-smoke campfire. Excess energy is sent to a USB port to charge small electronics. Even more impressive is that the same technology as well as the proceeds earned from CampStove sales are being used to help millions of people in developing countries. The larger BioLite HomeStove has been created as a clean alternative to cooking on smoky, open fires that negatively impact health and the environment, while charging life-improving devices such as mobile phones and LED lights.

WATER CHECKLIST

1

2

1. SANBORN CANOE CO.: The Enamel Camping Mug by Sanborn Canoe Company is built to last generations. Handmade in Poland, renowned for its quality enamelware, the nostalgic cup is the perfect companion for your outdoor adventures. ___2. DULUTH PACK: Large and square to fit easily in the bottom of a canoe, made of heavy canvas and closed by leather straps and buckles: little has changed in the design of a Duluth pack since Camille Poirier in Duluth, Minnesota patented his design in 1882. For over 100 years the company Duluth Pack has produced the iconic canoe pack that shares its name and seen its appeal extend from passionate outdoorsmen to urban adventurers of all ages.

1

2

3

1. ORU KAYAK: For kayak lovers with limited storage space, the Oru Kayak neatly folds up into its own carrying case with space for a paddle and more. ___ 2. NORQUAY CO.: Not only will Norquay paddles give you a smooth cruise around the lake, they are beautiful enough to hang on your wall. Made from 100% cherry wood. Pictured here are the Norquay beavertail paddles in the patterns Raw Hide and Forest Green. ___ 3. STANLEY: Heritage brands Stanley and Filson partnered for the commemorative Stanley Classic 100th Anniversary Bottle, issued in iconic hammertone green and accompanied by a tin cloth and bridle leather shoulder sling by Filson with adjustable shoulder strap for comfortable carrying.

1. PENDLETON: The Thomas Kay Scented Candle Collection by Oregon based Pendleton and New York fragrance design company Joya pay invoke Pendleton's outdoor heritage with the aromas of Cedar & Suede, Wood Smoke, and Mission Chai. Made from soy and beeswax, the candles come packaged in Pendleton fabric pouches in Thomas Kay patterns, paying homage to Pendleton's Scottish founder who came to Oregon in 1863. ___ 2. BOKER: There is more to this multipurpose black pen than meets the eye: the Tactical Pen by Boker is not only a high quality writing tool with a sturdy clip, screw-on cap, and comfortable finger groves; it also has a glass breaker tip in case of emergency, and can be used as a kubotan for self defense. ___3. KELLY KETTLE: A great design never goes out of style. For four generations, the Kelly family in Ireland has made boiling water in the outdoors quick and easy with its biomass-burning Kelly Kettle, a portable double-walled water boiler and cook stove. The principle of the "volcano kettle" is simple: water in the outside chamber is heated by the fire contained in the base. The center chamber acts like a chimney, drawing up hot air as the kettle heats, which then boils the water. The hot air from the chimney can also be used to prepare food with the Kelly Kettle pot support on top of the kettle and the lid which doubles as a cooking pot. Available in three sizes and in aluminum or stainless steel. ___4. ÁETEM: Ultimate multitasker in the range of seatrekking packs by German start-up Áetem. The carbon fiber Sea Shell "Charles D" keeps your pack dry and afloat while you explore the ocean, doubles as a bodyboard for catching waves, and with the simple addition of optional wheels can be transformed into a trolley as you roll through the airport towards your next adventure.

1. ORTLIEB: To keep your supplies dry, the Ortlieb Compression Dry Bag with Valve is an efficient and lightweight solution. Expelling air through the valve reduces packing volume to a minimum, while the nylon fabric PS 10 is ultra lightweight and robust. Ortlieb's signature roll closure with stiffening bar makes the pack easy to handle. ___ 2. PENDLETON: Made from 86% wool and 14% cotton, the Pendleton Yakima Camp Blanket offers rugged and stylish warmth both outdoors and indoors. Pair it with a Leather Blanket Carrier and you are good to go. ___ 3. PENDLETON: Pendleton approached fellow Oregonian Wood&Faulk to create the Thomas Kay Camp Stool. A classic essential, it features hardwood ash legs with brass hardware, a leather seat covered in Pendleton jacquard, and a detachable leather carrying strip.

First Aid Kit

100feet
（約30メートル）

GAS
250

WATER
TREATME
DROPS   PART A   PART B

Jun Oson

Index

Jun Oson

The Outsiders

New Outdoor Creativity

This book was conceived, edited, and designed by Gestalten.

Edited by Jeffrey Bowman, Sven Ehmann, and Robert Klanten
Text features by Jeffrey Bowman and Erling Kagge
Project descriptions and interviews by Alisa Kotmair

Cover and layout by Christian Schneider
Additional layout by Hendrik Hellige
Cover photography by David Boyson Cooper

Typefaces: Gill Facia by Eric Gill & Colin Banks,
Brandon Grotesque by Hannes von Döhren

Proofreading by Felix Lennert
Printed by Nino Druck GmbH, Neustadt / Weinstr.
Made in Germany

Published by Gestalten, Berlin 2014
ISBN 978-3-89955-513-4

3rd printing, 2015

For more information, please visit www.gestalten.com.

None of the content in this book was published in exchange for payment by commercial parties or designers; Gestalten selected all included work based solely on its artistic merit.

Bibliographic information published by the Deutsche Nationalbibliothek. The Deutsche Nationalbibliothek lists this publication in the Deutsche Nationalbibliografie; detailed bibliographic data are available online at http://dnb.d-nb.de.

This book was printed on paper certified by the FSC®.

Kilian Schönberger

Kilian Schönberger